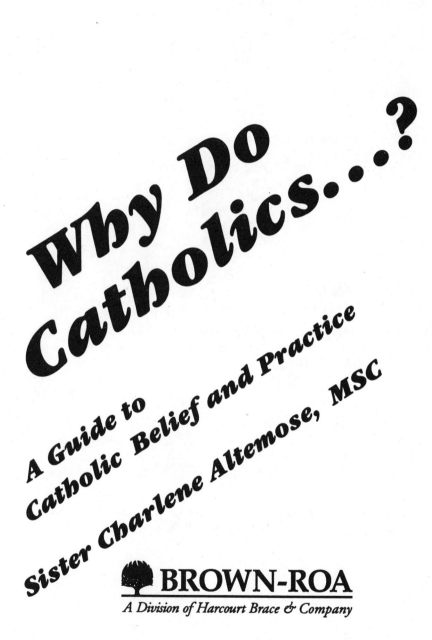

Why Do Catholics...?

A Guide to Catholic Belief and Practice

Sister Charlene Altemose, MSC

BROWN-ROA
A Division of Harcourt Brace & Company

Dubuque, Iowa

Book Team

Publisher—Ernest T. Nedder
Editorial Director—Sandra Hirstein
Production Editors—Karla A. McCarey and Marilyn Bowers Gorun
Production Manager—Marilyn Rothenberger
Art Director—Cathy Frantz
Graphic Designer—Debra O'Brien
Illustrator—Terri Webb (pages 21, 32, 33, 48, 52, 67, 68, 104, 110, 117)
Illustrator—Beth Owens (page 70)

Scripture Sources
Good News Bible: The Bible in Today's English Version © 1976 by
the American Bible Society.
The New American Bible © 1970 by the Confraternity of Christian
Doctrine, Washington, D.C.
The New Jerusalem Bible © 1985 by Darton, Longman & Todd, Ltd.
and Doubleday & Company, Inc.

Dedication

This book is lovingly dedicated to Mom and Dad who gifted
me with faith and love and to Father William P. Dodd who
helped me grow in faith.

ISBN 0–697–02690–6

13 12 11

Contents

iv

Acknowledgments

The writing of this book took me on a journey into my faith as I trod the paths of older truths and gathered the heritage of Catholic life in the light of Vatican II. As I traveled through the various phases, I recalled all those who have had a hand in this endeavor. I acknowledge my parents and teachers who instilled Catholic values in me from my earliest days.

As a Missionary Sister of the Sacred Heart, I owe gratitude to my religious community, who has provided my education and allowed me time to pursue this work, and who gave me their prayers, interest, and encouragement along the way.

I especially am grateful to the sisters at Sacred Heart Hospital, Allentown, who lived through each stage of this book with me.

My years at Alvernia College, Reading, Pennsylvania, enabled me to glean experience and depth through the courses I taught.

To the priests and people of St. Anne's Church in Bethlehem, Pennsylvania, I owe thanks for providing a community of faith in which I had the opportunity to explain and explore our faith.

I share the sentiments of Ralph Waldo Emerson who said of his friends, "The glory of friendship lies in spiritual inspiration that comes when one discovers that someone believes in him and is willing to trust him." To all my many friends: Thanks.

To Anne and Charles Gerras, who have so graciously shared their publishing expertise, guidance, and direction, I offer special appreciation.

Finally, I thank Sandra Hirstein and the editors of BROWN Publishing—ROA Media for their openness and willingness to listen and trust this endeavor.

Introduction

This volume, like Catholicism, has Jewish origins. The rabbi brought his Bar Mitzvah class to our parish church to learn more about Catholicism and to see the inside of a Catholic church.

Since it was a new experience for these twelve year olds, they stepped into the foyer wide-eyed and wary as if they were entering a haunted house. As they spied the picture of the pope with his white skull cap and cassock, one astute lad noted, "Look. He's wearing a yarmulke and prayer shawl."

I explained why we dip our fingers into the holy water font at the entrance. "We also purify ourselves and wash before we pray," they said. "And we bless," they noted, referring to the mezuzah which Jews touch when they enter their homes.

These Jewish students became intrigued by familiar customs and symbols. The tabernacle reminded them of the Ark in the synagogue which houses the Torah. The lectern and altar were like the Bimah, the table or platform-like dais on which the Torah is spread as it is read. "You also have a Ner Tamid (eternal light)," one lad observed when he saw the sanctuary lamp burning in front of where the Eucharist is reserved. The vigil light stand, with its glowing candles, was similar to the Yahrzeit plaque in the synagogue, inscribed with the names of those who died and lit on one's death anniversary. The multibranched candlestick resembled the menorah.

I told them how we worship and what we do at Mass. They noted that the liturgy format was much like their synagogue service. Similar themes were present in both the Mass and the Jewish service.

In both, the worshippers begin with an intention to praise by a "call to prayer." The people ask God for forgiveness for sins and shortcomings. God is given glory; Scripture is read. Faith is professed by Catholics in the Creed, by Jews in the Shema.

These enthusiastic Jewish students recognized their common Jewish blessing as similar to the Preparation of the Gifts prayer: "Blessed are you, Lord, God of all creation. . . ." Water, bread, and wine also play a role in their faith and are familiar symbols.

We arrived at the point where similarities ceased, but not their questions. "Why? What does that mean? When did it begin? Do all Catholics believe that?" they asked, as I explained reconciliation, the stations of the cross, devotion to Mary and the saints, the place of statues, and other Catholic customs.

It was an enriching, learning experience on both sides. Many Catholic customs trace their origins to Jewish practices. After all, Jesus was Jewish and so were the first Christians who translated their Jewish faith into another frame of reference in their Christian rituals.

I continued to ask questions as I pursued Catholic practices and the reasons behind the deeper meanings. Over the years, I have shared this approach with college students, catechists, catechumens, adults, and young people. I have discovered that the faith is more appreciated and loved when practices are seen in their historic setting and context.

In compiling this material, I owe a debt of gratitude to the many who spurred me on in my search by asking "Why?" In order to respond, I needed to delve into the traditions of our past. Historical circumstances have affected the way we have lived out our faith. Knowing the "How" and "Why" of changes helps us toward a more meaningful understanding of Catholicism.

Purpose and Approach

This book serves as an informative, objective explanation of the background and meaning of our Catholic practices, beliefs, and customs in the light of Vatican II renewal. I have attempted to present this material by beginning with externals and proceeding toward the inner spirit and attitudes. By no means do I believe this work is all-inclusive. However, I have tried to explain those aspects of Catholicism which are vital as well as those issues which I feel are important.

For this reason, I have opened with a discussion of the Catholics of the Eastern Rites, who for many Roman Catholics remain an enigma and are not recognized for their place in the faith. I then consider other externals: the papacy, the parish, Catholic worship, sacraments, and devotions, as practiced in the Latin Rite. The latter third of the book deals with inner qualities and attitudes: morality, prayer life, beliefs, and tolerance toward other religions.

This book will appeal to anyone who wants to know more about the Catholic Church, especially since Vatican II. It is for the catechumen who has made a faith-decision to become a Catholic, as well as for the cradle Catholic. It is for all those who are ready to ask deeper questions about Catholicism. This volume clarifies the image of the Church for those whose ideas are fashioned by the press and films, which often present misleading stereotypes of what Catholicism is all about.

Questions about Catholicism today cannot be answered in a matter-of-fact way. The response, "We do it just because we always did it that way," no longer satisfies thinking believers. Vatican II has challenged Catholics to a more responsible, meaningful, and faith-filled approach to the exercise of their faith and traditions. This book is a practical response to that challenge.

Second Vatican Council

Before we begin, let me answer a very basic question that all readers of this book will want to understand: What is the Second Vatican Council?

"The Second Vatican Council," "Vatican II," and "Ecumenical Council" are Catholic household words. Thanks to television, almost everyone has heard them.

Since the terms are used repeatedly in this book, we offer here an explanation as to why the Council is so important in the lives of Catholics, and significant to the world as well. Neither the Church nor the world has been the same since Vatican II, because the Council brought changes which affected how the Church and the world interact.

Never has any religious body undergone such a radical renewal in so short a time as has the Catholic Church since Vatican II. Ever since the Reformation in the sixteenth century, the Church had tended to close in on itself, to distance itself from "the world." Efforts at reform of this stance were never very effective. While isolated movements and individuals sought change, their attempts were not universally supported by Church leaders.

Institutional change required the vision and insight of Pope John XXIII, who perceived the direction of the Spirit and, in 1959, announced that he would convene an ecumenical (worldwide) council.

After preliminaries and much in-depth preparation, the pope called together all the bishops of the world and many Protestant and Orthodox observers for the Twenty-first Ecumenical Council. They met in Rome in four major sessions between 1962 and 1965.

Unlike other councils, whose aims were to proclaim doctrine and fend off heresy, Vatican II sought to make the Church meaningful and relevant to the twentieth century. The Council aimed to present the Church as a pastoral presence of Christ in the world and to work toward greater unity among all Churches. Openness, flexibility, change, and meaningfulness became the watchwords, expressed in Italian as *aggiornamento,* which means "updating" or "renewal."

This assembly was called "Vatican II" because the First Vatican Council, held in 1870, was never formally adjourned, due to the Franco-Prussian War.

The bishops were not always in agreement. Factions formed. Some thought the Church was not moving fast enough, while others saw no need for so much change. After four years of discussion, the culmination of the Council's work was expressed in the sixteen documents of Vatican II. These documents are the Council's official guidelines as to how the Church is to respond to its mission in the world today.

After two decades of implementing the documents, much change has taken place and still continues. The Council's efforts to put the faith within the grasp of ordinary people has brought a new life and vitality into the Catholic Church. The challenge remains to continue to develop a consistently deeper faith life, emphasizing the demands of the Spirit over legal demands and ritual exactness. Throughout this book, we will look at the Church in the light of the teachings of the Second Vatican Council. At times, we will regress to see where we have been in order to know where we are today.

I have written this book for lay persons, who are not so much concerned with theological nuances as they are with making the faith meaningful. They ask "Why . . . ?" I have tried to give some answers to help toward a greater appreciation of our heritage and traditions.

I

What Is the Catholic Church and Who Belongs to It?

Eastern Rites—Latin Rite— Eparchates—Icons

Introduction

The Catholic Church traces its origins to Jesus, his twelve apostles, and the first community of believers in Jerusalem. To understand Catholicism, it is important to know something about the diverse religious expressions which it includes. Although the Church is united in doctrines, beliefs, and leadership, Catholics carry out their faith and worship in a variety of liturgical expressions called Rites.

Most people are familiar with the largest Rite of the Catholic Church which is called the **Latin,** Western, or Roman **Rite.** But the Church also includes a number of ancient and vital **Eastern Rites,** whose existence and heritage cannot be ignored. This chapter deals with the notion of Rites and their origins. We then examine the specific theological perspectives and practices which are unique to the Eastern Church.

Rites: Concept and Origins

After Pentecost, the Good News of Jesus spread rapidly through Mediterranean lands. Zealous missionaries, such as **Paul** and **Barnabas,** formed small communities of faith who worshipped and prayed together.

Gradually, each community developed its own pattern of worship, with variations for the local Church. There evolved specific liturgical expressions flavored by customs and needs of a particular area. This is an early example of how Rites would develop.

The **Persecutions** (64–303) did not dampen the faith of the early Christians. Being forced underground, they practiced their beliefs with greater fervor. In 313, Emperor **Constantine** issued the **Edict of Milan** which established religious tolerance toward Christians. The Christians, in fear no more, built churches to accommodate the growing numbers and worshipped freely with cultural variations. Christianity became the official religion, and, within a few years, Alexandria, Antioch, and Rome thrived as centers of Christians, but each had its unique interpretations of how to worship.

Barnabas   *Missionary companion of St. Paul*

Constantine   *Roman emperor who gave religious freedom to Christians in* A.D. *313*

Eastern Rites   *Catholic Churches in union with Rome, but having liturgies and prayers specific to the particular Rite*

Edict of Milan   *Decree by Emperor Constantine granting religious freedom to Christians*

Latin Rite   *Western or Roman Rite of the Catholic Church; Catholic Churches with the Roman liturgy*

Paul   *Early convert to Christianity, apostle to the Gentiles*

Persecutions   *Local or general oppression of early Christians*

When Constantine moved his capital from Rome to a more central location, Byzantium (later called Constantinople), the Christian rituals of that area took on a distinct cultural flavor.

The Church developed along two divergent lines: East and West. The emperor and the bishop of Constantinople, who was called a patriarch, shared the leadership in the East. But the bishop of Rome acted as both a civil and religious leader in the West. Newly established local Churches in the West looked to Rome for direction, because Rome was the West's prime religious center. For this reason, worship in the West was modeled upon the Roman expression, which gradually came to be known as the Roman (or Latin) Rite.

On the other hand, newly established Churches in the Eastern Empire assimilated the languages and customs of a number of strong local Churches. Alexandria, Antioch, and Byzantium thrived both as urban centers and centers of Christianity. Their worship forms came to be known as the **Alexandrian, Antiochian,** and **Byzantine Rites.**

The East and the West differed on more than leadership and language. Increasing disagreements in theology and ideology were compounded by personality conflicts. Moreover, spirituality in the East and West had distinctly different flavors. The East concentrated on the mystical and symbolic approach to faith. The West stressed properness and uniformity.

This difference in perspective, along with political and geographic preferences, split Christianity in 1054 into the **Eastern Orthodox Church** and the **Western Roman Catholic Church.** While the majority of Eastern Orthodox Christians did not seek

Alexandrian Rite   *Early Eastern Rite based in Alexandria in Egypt*

Antiochian Rite   *Early Eastern Rite based in Antioch in Syria (Asia Minor)*

Byzantine Rite   *Early Eastern Rite based in Byzantium (Constantinople), Greece*

Eastern Orthodox Church   *Church of the East more or less centered in Constantinople, not in union with Rome*

Roman Catholic Church   *Church of the West centered in Rome when the Eastern Orthodox Church separated*

reconciliation with the Western Church, efforts at rapprochement and unity were not entirely futile. Some of the Eastern Rite Churches continued to recognize the pope of Rome as their spiritual leader or returned to union with Rome at a later date. And so the Eastern branch of the Catholic Church, that is, those Churches which recognize the authority of the pope, form the Catholic Churches of the Eastern Rites and are sometimes called **Uniates.**

These Eastern Rite Catholics differ from the Eastern Orthodox in regard to their choice of highest authority. Eastern Catholics follow the pope and their respective Eastern Rite bishops, or patriarch. Eastern Orthodox consider their Orthodox patriarch as their spiritual leader. They regard the pope, not as a supreme head over all bishops, but as bishop of Rome, "one among equals."

While Eastern Churches united with Rome are sometimes called Uniates, it is more accurate to call them "Catholic Churches of the Eastern Rites." In the **Roman Curia,** the office which deals with Eastern Rites is The Sacred Congregation of Oriental Churches.

There are eighteen different Eastern Rites, with about twelve million Catholics throughout the world. In the United States, there are 511,000 Catholics of Eastern Rites in eleven **eparchates,** the majority of whom belong to the Byzantine Rite.

Rituals and Practices of the Eastern Churches

The rituals of the Eastern Churches mirror a specific understanding and concept of God. The Divinity is transcendent and majestic. All communication with God, therefore, is expressed with solemnity and awe, and marked with mystical and symbolic celebrations. All externals of Eastern worship have an aura of transcendence and mystery about them.

Eparchate/Eparchy   *Eastern Church diocese*

Roman Curia   *The body of officially organized agencies assisting the pope in governing and administering the Church*

Uniates   *Eastern Rite Churches in union with Rome*

One can easily identify an Eastern church by its unique architecture: onion-shaped domes and triple-barred crosses: ☨ The rounded cupolas signify heaven and God's overall presence. The crosses, whose meaning has been lost in antiquity, are used by both Orthodox and Eastern Rite Catholics. In fact, one cannot distinguish from externals or the liturgy whether an Eastern Church is Orthodox or in union with Rome. One finds out by asking if the Church is Catholic or Orthodox.

The church building itself is considered most sacred. It is where God most intimately meets people and heaven is joined to earth. Upon entering an Eastern church, one is struck by the vivid gold, blue, and red which dominate the decor. To a Westerner, the decor may seem excessive, but to the Easterner, it symbolizes the splendor and majesty of God.

Icons

After noting the color scheme, your attention most likely will be drawn to the ornate partition which separates the nave from the sanctuary in many Eastern Rite churches. The icon screen or **iconostasis** is a large, wooden screen on which are paintings of Christ, the Mother of God, angels, and saints.

To understand Eastern theology, one must consider the central role that **icons** play in the faith life of the Eastern believer. Icons are not mere art forms or decorations; they symbolize the deepest realities of faith. The icon screen does not display images for their own sake, but represents the mysteries of salvation history.

Christ, the Mother of God, John the Baptist, and the patron saint of the particular Church appear in a specific order, and show the ways that God and all humankind have been joined.

Icon   *Two-dimensional religious painting proper to the Eastern Rite Churches*

Iconostasis   *Large, wooden screen painted with icons; separates the nave from the sanctuary in many Eastern Rite churches*

The **Royal Doors,** the gateway leading into the sanctuary, represent the Kingdom of God. The icons above the doorway depict Christ's presence in the world as man, in the Eucharist, and in the Scriptures, as portrayed by icons of the annunciation, the Last Supper, and the evangelists.

Since the sanctuary is blocked from view and since one enters only through the Royal Doors, the icon screen is a "window of heaven." The sanctuary represents the spiritual and the nave symbolizes the earth.

The artistic style of icons with elongated faces, bold piercing eyes, and large hands is used to symbolize the spiritual, which reaches beyond time. Icons are reverenced, but not worshipped. On entering the church, an Eastern Christian kisses the icon screen images in a specific order.

An icon painter understands that he or she is engaged in a sacred craft and prepares for the task by prayer and fasting. An artist is not free to exercise individuality. Each icon must be a copy of another which already exists and has a long tradition of being miraculous.

Since all realms of creation praise God, the icon contains elements of each. An icon is painted on specially blessed wood, the contribution of the plant world. The mineral world is represented in the chalk or alabaster which is used to smooth the wood. Egg-based paints signify the gift of the animal kingdom. The hands of the artisan express the human and spiritual. Thus, in an icon, heaven and earth join together in praise of God.

Worship

The main act of worship, called the **Divine Liturgy,** preserves the most ancient rituals of Christianity. The atmosphere breathes majesty and mystery, and time assumes a sacred character. Time ceases when one adores God, just as time assumed another dimension when Christ was born. And so the period of worship may seem unduly long for those not accustomed to Eastern ways. Solemn processions, incense, elaborate vestments, and lengthy music selections evoke awe and reverence.

Divine Liturgy   *The main act of worship in Eastern Rite (Catholic and Orthodox) Churches*

Royal Doors   *Gateway to the sanctuary in an iconostasis (wooden screen) in an Eastern Rite church*

Because humans are the living instruments of God, all music is rendered without the aid of instruments. This *a capella* feature is the pride of the Eastern Church and even the smallest parish boasts an excellent choir.

Although the Eastern Liturgy contains the basic elements of a Latin Rite Mass, a Western Rite Catholic may find the liturgy difficult to follow because of the unfamiliar language and ceremonies.

Eastern Liturgy represents an encounter with the risen Lord through the power of the Spirit, so the attitude during worship is solemn joy and awesome mystery. Worshippers in Eastern Churches stand during most of the liturgy as a sign of respect. They show their deepest respect by bowing. Genuflecting or bending the knee is not customary.

The sign of the cross capsulizes the great mysteries of faith. The first three fingers are joined as a unit to symbolize the Trinity. The last two fingers, bent into the center of the palm, represent Jesus as God and human. As these two fingers point to oneself, so Jesus comes into one's life. One truly can be called a child of God. Eastern Christians sign themselves by touching the forehead, chest, right shoulder, and then the left. This differs from the Western gesture which involves first signing the left shoulder. The Eastern way symbolizes Jesus sitting at the right hand of God, and so the right is signed first.

Mysteries

What the Latin Church calls sacraments are mysteries in the Eastern Church. While in essence the same, they differ in externals and theological emphasis.

Baptism, which admits one to the faith, is followed by confirmation **(chrismation)** the sealing of baptism in the Spirit, and by Communion. These Sacraments of Initiation establish a total rebirth and so are given at the same time.

Eastern Rite Catholics have their own clergy who are ordained by the respective patriarchs. Eastern Church regulations regarding celibacy differ from the Roman Church rules. "Eastern Rite candidates for Holy Orders may marry before becoming deacons, and may

Chrismation   *Confirmation in the Eastern Rite Churches, received with baptism and first Eucharist*

continue in marriage thereafter, but marriage after ordination is forbidden. In the U.S., Eastern Rite bishops do not ordain married candidates for the priesthood."[1]

Eastern Churches are divided into eparchates under the authority of the bishop who is called an **eparch.**

Inter-Ritual Regulations

Although it is customary to worship in one's own Rite, a Roman Catholic may validly attend the Divine Liturgy and receive Communion in an Eastern Catholic Church or from a priest of an Eastern Catholic Rite.

Some Catholic priests hold faculties to celebrate the liturgy in both the Eastern and Western Rites. Since 1971, priests of Latin and Eastern Rites may concelebrate in the Rite of the host Church.

In a marriage between Latin and Eastern Rite Catholics, the wedding takes place in the church of the bride, but the new family usually is expected to follow the Rite of the husband and father. To change Rites requires the permission of the respective bishop.

Vatican II upheld the ancient traditions and recognized the equality of the Eastern Church and the Latin Church. The "Decree on Eastern Catholic Churches" states: "Such individual Churches whether of the East or of the West, although they differ somewhat among themselves in what are called rites (that is, in liturgy, ecclesiastical discipline, and spiritual heritage) are, nevertheless, equally entrusted to the pastoral guidance of the Roman Pontiff. . . . They are consequently of equal dignity, so that none of them is superior to the others by reason of rite."[2]

The Catholics of Eastern Rites preserve a vital link between East and West. To visit an Eastern Church, whether Catholic or Orthodox, broadens horizons and allows persons to experience their faith from another perspective. Total unity between Orthodoxy and Roman Catholicism is still to be seen, but the glory and heritage of the East shines in the West through the Eastern Churches united to Rome.

---

1. Felician Foy, O.F.M., ed. *Catholic Almanac* (Huntington, Indiana: Our Sunday Visitor, 1986), p. 300.

2. Walter M. Abbott, S.J., ed. "Decree on Eastern Catholic Churches," *The Documents of Vatican II* (New York: America Press, 1966), p. 374, article 3.

Eparch   *Bishop of an eparchate*

Rites of the Catholic Church

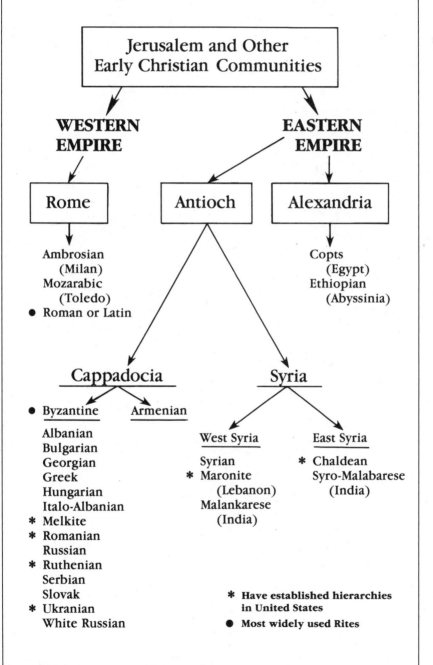

Jerusalem and Other
Early Christian Communities

WESTERN EMPIRE

EASTERN EMPIRE

Rome

Antioch

Alexandria

Ambrosian
(Milan)
Mozarabic
(Toledo)
● Roman or Latin

Copts
(Egypt)
Ethiopian
(Abyssinia)

Cappadocia

Syria

● Byzantine   Armenian

Albanian
Bulgarian
Georgian
Greek
Hungarian
Italo-Albanian
* Melkite
* Romanian
Russian
* Ruthenian
Serbian
Slovak
* Ukranian
White Russian

West Syria

Syrian
* Maronite
(Lebanon)
Malankarese
(India)

East Syria

* Chaldean
Syro-Malabarese
(India)

* Have established hierarchies
in United States
● Most widely used Rites

II

Why Do Catholics Have a Pope?

**Pope—Vicar of Christ—Papacy—
Vatican—College of Cardinals—Fourth
Lateran Council—Infallibility—Mary's
Assumption—Magisterium—Papal
States—Bishop—Cardinal—Diocese**

Introduction

The reverence and respect Catholics pay to the pope
often puzzles outsiders. Why do Catholics travel to the
Vatican to see the pope? Why do millions turn out to greet
him when he visits? Why is a rosary touched or blessed by
the pope a treasured memento?

This devotion may seem to be hero-worship or
fanaticism. But Catholics identify the pope with all that
one's faith represents. As **Vicar of Christ** and successor of
Peter, the pope serves as a tangible link between apostolic
times and today. The sacred roots and traditions of
Catholicism live on in the authority handed on from Christ
to Peter to the pope today.

Although Catholics may not always agree with the
pope, yet in their hearts lies the symbolic realization of
what the pope signifies. The papacy provides a unified
spiritual leader in the pope, and the hierarchical

organization guarantees security to carry on the mission of Christ in the world.

In this chapter, we examine the role of the pope and how it has evolved over the years. We also consider the structure and the administration of the Church on the Vatican and diocesan levels.

Historical Overview of the Papacy

Catholic understanding of the authority of the pope is based on the belief that Peter had special primacy and leadership throughout Jesus' public life. The tradition that Peter set up his see in Rome gave the bishop of Rome priority. Although several Scripture passages attest to Peter's leadership role, the passage, "You are Peter, and upon this rock I will build my Church. . . ." (see Matthew 16:13–19) is used most commonly as biblical evidence. Early Church history about the preeminence of the papal office is somewhat nebulous. But it is fair to state that in the first several hundred years of Christianity, the bishop of Rome exercised more authority than bishops of other Christian strongholds. Richard McBrien contends that the Church of Rome "intervened in the life of distant churches, took sides in theological controversies, was consulted by other bishops on doctrinal and moral issues." It also was the focal point of unity for all Churches.[1]

It was not until the Middle Ages that the pope as sole religious leader became evident. By A.D. 800, the title "papa" came into use. Popes were usually selected by the emperor, but at the **Fourth Lateran Council** in 1215, the **College of Cardinals** was established as the body which selected the pope.

1. Richard McBrien. *Catholicism* (San Francisco, California: Winston Press, Harper and Row Publishers, Inc., 1981), p. 832.

College of Cardinals   *The cardinals of the entire Church; a cardinal is called a "Prince of the Church" and is an elector of the Church unless retired (age eighty)*

Fourth Lateran Council   *The "Great Council," gathering of the pope and bishops in Rome in 1215; established Easter Communion practice, initiated a four-year truce for Christian nations, organized the College of Cardinals*

Vicar of Christ   *A title for the pope*

To trace the history of the **papacy** is to study Western Civilization, for history has been affected by the popes. They were central to all human endeavors. Popes made and enforced laws, waged wars, fought heresy, led Crusades, canonized saints, owned lands, and fought for the throne.

Neither was the papacy exempt from scandals. There have been about thirty anti-popes in Catholic Church history. These individuals claimed or exercised papal authority although they had not been duly elected. The anti-popes included those who reigned during the Western Schism (1377–1408) when rival popes reigned in Avignon, France, and in Rome. Popes have fathered illegitimate children and bought and sold the papal office, as well as spiritual favors. As overpowering landlords, some exploited the poor.

As disheartening as these facts may be, the papacy on the whole has been graced by devout, God-fearing, noble individuals. Although the leaders of the Reformation reacted drastically to the ignoble practices within the Church, the papacy sought stability through the Council of Trent. This Council, held from 1545 to 1563, upheld law and order, staunchly pursued truth, and emphasized papal authority.

The defensive posture endured for the next several centuries and climaxed during the First Vatican Council in 1870 with the dogma of papal infallibility.

Infallibility

This issue is most confusing and demands explanation. The pope speaks infallibly, that is, free from error, when he clearly states he is using his infallible authority. He must intend what he proclaims to be a matter of belief for the whole Church and it must concern faith and morals. The bishops share in this infallibility when, in union with the pope, they proclaim a dogma, either at an ecumenical council or with some other manner of teaching.

In reality, infallibility or *ex cathedra* teaching (from the chair of Peter) is rarely used. The last time an infallible dogma was declared was in 1950 with the proclamation of Mary's **Assumption** into heaven. The pope was proclaiming and affirming a truth which had been part of faith all along. By defining a truth infallibly, the pope puts the authoritative seal upon it and places that truth in the realm of *dogma.*

Assumption   *The dogma concerning Mary being assumed into heaven after death, body and soul*

Papacy   *The office of the pope*

The Papal Office and Collegiality

The popes continued to exercise their authority in the spirit of the First Vatican Council until 1959 when Pope John XXIII recognized the need for a radical shift in emphasis in order to relate more meaningfully to the world of modern times.

Vatican II, while effecting changes, recognized the pope as authoritative head of the Catholic Church. However, in keeping with the spirit of renewal, the pope's role since Vatican II has been exercised more often in communion with the other bishops in shared decision making called **collegiality.** The papal office has changed from that of a rigid dictator to benevolent apostle and pastor. The pope continues to work in collaboration with the bishops through the Synod of Bishops which meets to discuss pertinent issues.

The pope and bishops, as the highest teaching authority of the Church, are responsible for handing on the faith. They make up what is commonly known as the **magisterium,** the Church's teaching authority. They teach in a variety of ways: through ecumenical councils; encyclicals, which are issued by the pope on a specific issue; and upholding faith in what is called ordinary teaching, preserving the truths which are part of revelation.

The openness and dialogue begun with Vatican II continue in the pontificate of Pope John Paul II. He has taken the papacy beyond the confines of the Vatican to meet the world's peoples on their own soil. In his trips to remote areas, he has brought the saving power and presence of Christ to people of all faiths. The pope of today leads Catholics, but over and above, he is a powerful sign of Christ's hope for unity and peace, and a much-admired spiritual leader in the world.

Collegiality   *The union of all the world's bishops with the pope; often refers to the decision-making power of this group*

Magisterium   *The teaching authority of the Church*

Church Administration—
The Vatican

The central administration of the Catholic Church is located in the **Vatican,** 108 acres within the city of Rome. **Vatican City,** the world's smallest independent nation was established in 1929 through the Lateran Treaty. Prior to that time, the pope ruled the **Papal States** which comprised much of central Italy and were a remnant of the Holy Roman Empire. The Vatican issues its own stamps, has its own inner government, currency, broadcast and communications network, and newspaper.

Diplomatic ties with many nations are carried out through **Apostolic Nuncios** and **Apostolic Pronuncios,** who represent the pope as ambassadors. Representatives of the pope in countries with no diplomatic ties to the Vatican are exercised through **Apostolic Delegates.** An Apostolic Delegate has jurisdiction regarding ecclesial and religious matters over the Catholic Church in a particular nation.

Apostolic Delegate   *A papal representative with no diplomatic status*

Apostolic Nuncio   *Ambassador from the Vatican assigned to a predominantly Catholic country*

Apostolic Pronuncio   *Ambassador from the Vatican assigned to a country which is not predominantly or officially Catholic*

Papal States   *The temporary land holdings of the papacy prior to 1870; the last of the Papal States was formally signed over to Italy in 1929 with the Lateran Concordat*

Vatican   *The residence of the pope*

Vatican City   *Part of Rome designated by the Lateran Treaty of 1929 as an independent state, contains the central administration of the Catholic Church and the residence of the pope*

The **Swiss Guards** since 1500 have served as the pope's personal security and army. As they stand guard at the Vatican gates, the pope's soldiers are distinguished by the colorful striped uniforms designed by Michelangelo.

Vatican City is dominated by St. Peter's Basilica, the largest church in the world. The Vatican also contains the Vatican Palace; the Vatican Library, with many rare manuscripts; the Sistine Chapel; an astronomical observatory; and administrative offices.

The Roman Curia, existing since the twelfth century, is the central governing body for the entire Church. It has evolved into a vast network of commissions, bureaus, offices, and departments. It has been reorganized since Vatican II in keeping with renewal and ecclesial changes.

Next to the pope in authority are the **cardinals.** These are usually bishops who are appointed by the pope. Traditionally known as "Princes of the Church," the cardinals' main task is to assemble in conclave to select a pope. They also may serve in the Curia or a diplomatic post, or head a diocese. Collectively, they are the College of Cardinals.

Auxiliary Bishop *Assistant bishop in a diocese with no right of succession*

Cardinal *A bishop of high rank, an elector of the pope (until age eighty), a "Prince of the Church"*

Coadjutor Bishop *Assistant bishop in a diocese with the right of succession*

Crosier *Bishop's staff or walking stick, an insignia of the episcopal office*

Diocese *The territory under the jurisdiction of a bishop*

Miter *A hat with peaks in front and back, worn by a bishop at liturgical services*

Pectoral Cross *Cross on a chain worn by a bishop or an abbot as a sign of office*

Swiss Guards *The Vatican security force charged with the personal safety of the pope; members wear uniforms designed by Michelangelo*

Local Church Administration— Diocese and Bishop

The Church throughout the world is divided into **dioceses,** fully organized ecclesiastical jurisdictions. The head of the diocese, the bishop, has jurisdiction in his realm. The pope, as the bishop of Rome, is a direct successor of Peter, the apostle, and he thus preserves a historical connection in continuing the mission of Jesus. A bishop is appointed by the pope and ordained with the fullness of holy orders, which gives him the power to ordain priests and to confirm. The bishop assigns clergy, administers church property, and oversees the Catholic faith and observance in his diocese.

At his ordination, he dons the red cassock and skull cap and the bishop's ring. For formal liturgical celebrations at which he presides, the bishop carries a **crosier** (shepherd's staff), wears a **miter,** which is a triangular headpiece, and a large ornamented **pectoral cross**—all of which symbolize his office.

The head of a diocese is an ordinary bishop. He may be assisted by another bishop who has the right of succession, the **coadjutor.** An assistant bishop without the right of succession is called an **auxiliary bishop.**

Miter   Crosier

Pectoral Cross

The bishop is assisted in governing his diocese by a **chancellor** and a **vicar general.** The chancellor, who need not be a cleric, is the notary of a diocese. He or she is in charge of all documents regarding government of the diocese, deeds, archives, dispensations, and ecclesiastical matters. The vicar general is a priest appointd by the bishop to aid in governing. He has jurisdictional authority, except in matters reserved for the bishop. The office of diocesan administration is the **chancery,** and the main church of the diocese is the **cathedral.** Priests assist in governing through the Senate of Priests, tribunals, and other offices.

Several dioceses in a geographical area work together; and the chief of these is called the **archdiocese.** The bishop who leads an archdiocese is called the **archbishop.** When several dioceses and archdioceses are joined into a unit they form a **province.**

However, the diocese remains the basic subdivision of the universal Church and is subject to the Vatican. Each bishop is required by law to report directly to the pope every five years on the status of his diocese.

From the previous explanation, it may seem that the Church is a gargantuan monolith. It gives that impression because the hierarchical structure of the Catholic Church is very visible. But the authority and structure, like a scaffold, hold the organization together and are most necessary. The heart and spirit and faith of Catholicism reaches far beyond its imposing external organization, as subsequent chapters will reveal.

Archbishop   *Usually the bishop of an archdiocese*

Archdiocese   *Usually a metropolitan see, the principal see in a province of dioceses*

Cathedral   *Principal church of a diocese, where the bishop has his seat*

Chancellor   *Notary of a diocese*

Chancery   *The office of administration for a diocese*

Province   *An archdiocese and one or more nearby dioceses*

Vicar General   *A priest or bishop appointed by the bishop of a diocese to act as his deputy in the diocesan administration*

Organization of the Roman Catholic Church

Network of Administrative Offices

ROMAN CURIA

Congregations

Doctrine of the Faith
Oriental Churches
Bishops
Sacraments and Divine
  Worship
Causes of Saints
Clergy
Seminaries and
  Institutes of Studies
Evangelization of
  Peoples
Institutes of
  Consecrated Life and
  Societies

Tribunals

Apostolic
  Penitentiary
Apostolic
  Signature
Roman Rota
  (Court of Appeal)

**Secretariat
of State**

Councils

Inter-religious
  Dialogue
Non-Believers
Christian Unity
Justice and Peace
Laity
Social Communications
Authentic
  Interpretation of the
  Code of Canon Law
Latin America
Spiritual Care of
  Migrants and
  Tourists
Cor Unum
Family
Culture

Hierarchy

Pope
Cardinals
Archbishops
Bishops
^
Ordinary
Coadjutor
Auxiliary

Geographical Divisions

Vatican
Provinces
Archdioceses
Dioceses (Sees)
Parishes

III

What Is the Local Community of Faith?

**Parish—Convent—Parochial School—
Rectory—Stations of the Cross—
Statues—Sanctuary—Tabernacle—
Genuflection—Lectionary**

Introduction

The Catholic Church visibly shows forth its faith and the working of the Spirit in the local community of faith, the **parish.** An active Catholic identifies with a specific community of believers joined to live the faith on a day-to-day basis. The parish is really the whole Church in miniature, throbbing with the same Spirit as the larger institution.

The parish, then, is the subject of this chapter. We deal first with the externals that are most clearly seen: the parish complex and types and variations in parishes. We then reflect on some of the qualities an ideal parish ought to portray in the spirit of Vatican II. In order to provide a deeper meaning for what we often take for granted, the parish church itself, we conclude the chapter with a tour of a typical church and what one may expect to find in a Catholic church. For those who have never been inside a Catholic church, it is information. And it is a refresher for Catholics who may not even be able to tell you the color of the walls. For everyone, the purpose of this chapter is to heighten awareness of the Church as it appears in our midst.

The Parish— Variations and Styles

The Catholic Church may seem totally uniform, but closer scrutiny soon shows that this is not the case, especially when considering the local parish. In size and character, in style and management, parishes are as varied as the colors of the spectrum. There are sprawling suburban parishes where worshippers by the thousands converge each Sunday after having traveled many miles and parking in stadium-sized parking lots. These congregants may be as mobile as their mode of transport.

There are inner city parishes, sandwiched between skyscrapers and suffering from urban blight. Their parishioners include the homeless, the victimized, the poor. Small rural parish churches dot the open prairies of the Midwest. There are intimate neighborhood parishes where generations of family members have worshipped. Each parish assumes the character of those who comprise it, since the parish basically is people. Parishes vary, too, according to size, location, ethnic origins, and leadership.

A parish is usually set up when there is sufficient evidence that a viable community of faith can flourish. A parish is given the name of a saint or a truth of faith, for example, Saint Joseph Parish or Holy Trinity Parish. Most often territorial with clearly defined boundaries, a parish is the responsibility of the pastor. The Catholic population is determined by a census of the area.

Ethnic parishes, established for persons of the same cultural background, nationality, and language were most prevalent when waves of immigrants settled in a particular neighborhood. The people retained their own language and customs of their native land.

Parish   *A community of the faithful, generally territorial and centered in a church building*

Today, ethnic parishes stemming from Europe are fading from the scene. However, there is a rise in Hispanic parishes, especially in urban centers and the Southwest. Sometimes, a parish is set up for a specific group of people at military bases or on college campuses. A mission parish is set up when there are enough parishioners to warrant a parish. There is no resident clergy, so a neighboring parish usually serves it.

The Parish Complex

The parish church is an important center for one's faith life. Here one is baptized, worships, marries, and from here one is buried. The parish attempts to minister to the spiritual needs of all its members.

The architectural style of a church reflects the faith for which it was built. Whether made of stone, brick, wood, marble, or clapboard, the parish church stands as a testimony of Christ present today. The pointed spires of church steeples dominate many skylines and are an ever-present reminder of people's need to turn to God in prayer, like hands folded in prayer. Churches also have been modeled on Greek and Roman temples with rounded domes and sturdy columns.

Architecture reflects the thinking of the times. And so, since Vatican II, the trend has turned to reverential simplicity or modern styles. For an interesting study, drive around your town and note the variations of architecture in all the churches.

The typical parish complex usually includes a **rectory,** the residence for the priests who serve the parish.

When immigration of Catholics was at its height, the education of the children received priority. In order to preserve and pass on the faith and to provide for a well-rounded education, **parochial schools** were set up by most parishes. In fact, the Third Plenary Council of Baltimore in 1884 ordered that, where possible, every parish Church should have a school.

Parochial School *A Catholic school, parish or diocesan owned and administered, sometimes a private school owned and/or administered by a religious community*

Rectory *Residence for priests*

Parochial schools usually have been staffed by sisters of teaching religious communities. They live in homes called **convents.**

However, the parochial school system, while still part of parish life, has undergone drastic change, due to rising costs, fewer vocations to the sisterhood, and government regulations, such as busing, certification requirements, and aid to private schools. Many schools have either closed completely or consolidated. Lay personnel make up the majority of parochial school staffs.

These changes ought not to be regarded as the demise of the parochial school system or a weakening of faith. Today, there still are about seven thousand parochial elementary schools in the United States.

Parishes also are becoming more aware of the need to provide for the continuing religious formation of all its people, not just its children. Adult education and continuing adult spiritual formation programs have received more attention in recent years.

In order to accommodate itself to the diverse needs in the Church, parishes may include an all-purpose community center in their plans with facilities to serve different and varied groups. The Scouts, Knights of Columbus, Rosary Society, Legion of Mary, Charismatic Prayer Group, Bible Study Group, Holy Name Society, and Sodality—all may find space to gather in the parish facilities. A parish reaches beyond its boundaries to the needs of the community. You may find a day-care center, food bank, Alcoholics Anonymous room, shelter for the homeless, a thrift shop, or library facilities.

Parish Life

The parish complex is but the tangible aspect of parish life. But it is what most easily identifies what is Catholic. A parish, which is visible in the community, is usually a beehive of activity and an authentic witness for the cause of Christ. And so the ultimate test of a dynamic living parish lies in its never having quite enough room or time, for there are always needs to be filled.

But the parish is not essentially externals; it is an attitude and inner spirit which pervades throughout. Let us reflect on some of the qualities which mark a parish in tune with Vatican II.

Convent   *Residence for women religious*

Since it is through the parish that one worships in community, everyone needs to experience a sense of belonging. A parish striving to be a dynamic sign of Christ's presence has no place for cliques or prejudice. Rather, through the common expression of faith, a spirit of fellowship and warmth is evident. The parish is where parishioners and visitors feel at home, even if they may not know each other on a familiar basis.

Another salient feature in parish life today lies in the quality of leadership. Priests and all parish personnel in charge of some phase of parochial activities need to exhibit a sense of dedication coupled with caring, compassion, and understanding toward all.

Because the most common way a parish joins in a communal experience is through worship, liturgical celebrations ought to demonstrate the depth of faith. The laity are entitled to be provided with sufficient direction toward intelligent and meaningful participation in the liturgy and sacraments. Challenging homilies and adequate explanation about changes and ritual customs also contribute to understanding.

A parish alive with the Spirit provides opportunities of ongoing formation for all its members. This can take the form of adult education, youth ministry, parish renewal programs, or the provision for individual spiritual direction. Parish retreats, whether conducted on successive evenings or on weekends supply the experience of shared faith in small groups, and lead to deeper spiritual insights.

The parish is people, and when love and concern for each other are united with involvement, generosity, and support of the parish, one cannot doubt that the spirit of Vatican II thrives among the parishioners. Likewise, in the spirit of Christ, the care extends beyond parish walls and reaches out to all in need.

Inside a Catholic Church

We enter the church through the foyer which is called a **vestibule.** In years gone by, when people walked to church, this area served as a shelter from the elements as well as a gathering place. Announcements and reading material also are available here. Since Vatican II, the vestibule serves liturgical functions: a vesting place for the priest and the starting point for the Entrance Procession on Sundays and feast days.

Vestibule   *Foyer and entrance to a church*

When a Catholic steps into the church, he or she dips his or her fingers into a holy water font at the door and blesses himself or herself. This gesture not only has its origins in the ancient practice of purification before prayer, but it serves as a reminder of one's baptism. In making the sign of the cross, a Catholic ought to also renew one's baptismal commitment in his or her heart.

Some churches have preserved the ancient custom of remembering the poor and less fortunate, by providing a **poor box** at the entrance. It is in keeping with the custom of the early Christians who "shared all things in common." (Acts 2:44)

The **nave** of the church, where the congregants gather for worship, ordinarily is equipped with pews and kneelers which are arranged either in rows or in a circle around the altar. In large cathedrals or basilicas, the nave may be bare and have room for standing. Today some churches also use movable furniture to accommodate different sizes of congregations.

Church decor varies. It may be decorated in striking bold colors, subdued pastels, or plain plaster. Paneling, murals, frescoes, marble columns, mosaics, or wooden beams are a few of the many options for interior church designs.

No matter what the decor, the church is pervaded by an air of reverence and quiet, which is conducive to prayer. This is partly due to the lighting effects. Since the Middle Ages, multicolored **stained-glass windows** have been used in churches to add to the devotion. The exquisite artistry of Bible scenes and saints etched in glass provided meaningful visual aids for the commoners who were illiterate. The stained-glass windows were often called the "Bible of the Poor." Modern churches still use stained glass, but often they are designed with contemporary liturgical symbols.

The fourteen **stations of the cross,** which portray the Passion and death of Jesus, adorn the walls or back of the church. These stations usually are plaques, statues, or simple crosses. Early Christians

Nave   *Main body of a church building*

Poor Box   *Collection box at church entrance for alms for the less fortunate*

Stained-glass Windows   *Colorful windows often found in churches; many tell biblical stories or depict saints, others are symbolic*

Stations of the Cross   *A series of meditations on the sufferings, death, and burial of Christ*

traced the steps of Christ in Jerusalem during his Passion. After the Moslems conquered the Holy Land, the pilgrimages temporarily ceased, and "stations" were placed in churches as a pious devotion. In 1731, the general features of the stations became uniform and special blessings and indulgences were attached to meditating on Christ's Passion. In order to complete the Paschal Mystery theology, some parishes have unofficially added a fifteenth station, resurrection.

Statues of saints or angels may be on a pedestal, in a niche, or on a side altar. Vatican II placed emphasis on liturgy and the sacraments, and so devotions to the saints take a secondary position in a Catholic's faith life. That is why there are fewer statues in modern churches or even a lack of them. However, statues of Mary, St. Joseph, the Sacred Heart of Jesus, and St. Anthony retain their popularity.

Vigil lights, glass vials containing candles or, in line with modern technology, small electric lights triggered when a coin is put into the slot, may burn before the statues or in a separate stand. A candle is lit to pray for a special intention or for the soul of a loved one. Catholics believe prayers can assist the dead who are in **purgatory** to atone for their sins. A candle, too, symbolizes a constant presence. One's prayers continue through the light left burning when we cannot be present.

To an outsider, the most foreboding and curious feature of a Catholic church is the **confessional.** This darkened alcove where one "goes to confession" has often been a stumbling block for prospective converts. The shift in theology of Vatican II aimed to make the confessional less ominous, although private confession of sin still is a vital aspect of Catholic belief and practice.

The Sacrament of Reconciliation today is meant to be a healing experience of the compassionate Christ, and so one no longer needs to confess in the darkness of the confessional. One can opt for a face-to-face confession in which the person who confesses faces the priest

Confessional *Darkened alcove in a church for confession with a screen between the priest and penitent*

Purgatory *Place or condition of temporal suffering and punishment for those who have died in the state of grace, but with some attachment to sin*

Statues *Three-dimensional representations of Jesus, Mary, the saints, or angels; often found in churches, but away from the main altar*

and, in an informal way, asks to be forgiven and healed. To accommodate this option, churches have **reconciliation rooms** with soft chairs and ample lighting.

Some churches also make room for both preferences by a creative innovation. The confessional has been altered so that one side can be used for traditional closed-box, anonymous confessions, and the other side with the screen removed is replaced with a comfortable chair and light for face-to-face confessions.

In most churches, a separate place is reserved for baptisms. This **baptistry** can either be a simple font with a bowl or a separate room. Baptism is usually done by pouring water on the head. But baptism by immersion, in which the person is briefly submerged in water, is permitted, and some churches may have a pool-like baptistry.

Baptistry   *The place for administering baptisms, often near an entrance to a church or near the sanctuary and altar*

Reconciliation Room   *Small room for the celebration of the Sacrament of Reconciliation, set up for face-to-face confession, though a screen is sometimes available*

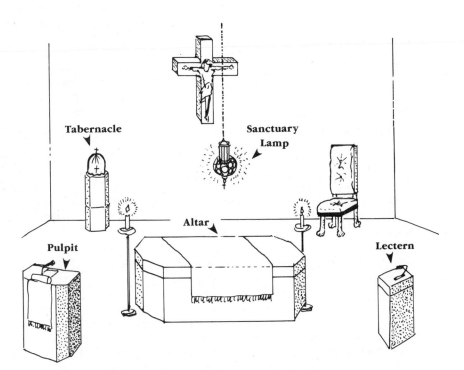

Tabernacle

Sanctuary Lamp

Altar

Pulpit

Lectern

The most sacred and focal point in a Catholic church is the **sanctuary,** where the liturgy is offered. An altar is the chief furnishing in the sanctuary. It is elevated and faces the people, either in the front of the church or in the center with pews surrounding it. The altar is the table of the Lord's Supper and the sacrifice. It is unadorned when not in use. Within the sanctuary, chairs for the celebrants and participants, a pulpit, and a lectern hold prominent positions.

The **tabernacle** contains consecrated hosts which are used at Communion or taken to the sick. This cabinet-like receptacle is kept locked and secured. A **sanctuary lamp** burns continuously before the tabernacle, to remind us of Christ's sacramental presence. A

Sanctuary   *The portion of the church building that contains the altar*

Sanctuary Lamp   *A candle or lamp that is kept burning before the Blessed Sacrament*

Tabernacle   *The structure in which the Blessed Sacrament is reserved, sometimes at a side altar or a separate chapel*

Catholic shows respect for the Eucharist by **genuflecting** on one knee or bowing when one passes the tabernacle or enters the pew.

The Word of God is an essential part of Catholic faith. The **Lectionary** is carried solemnly at the entrance procession, incensed at solemn occasions, and enthroned in a prominent place in the sanctuary.

A room called the **sacristy** which means "holy place," is where the sacred vessels, vestments, and other items used during liturgy are prepared and stored. In a small sink, the **sacrarium,** the sacred vessels are washed after being used at Mass.

Music has always played an important role in worship. The choir area, in a loft or at the front, back, or side of the church is usually dominated by the organ. With the liturgical renewal, other instruments, such as guitars, flutes, violins, trumpets, pianos, and electronic keyboards have come into use.

Art works and other symbols which enhance one's faith are appropriate in a church setting.

Other facilities to serve specific needs also may be provided. Some churches supply a crying room, fitted with a glass front, for parents and babies. Ramps and pews reserved for those in wheelchairs make it possible for the disabled to join in worship. This is all in an effort to be sensitive to the needs of others.

These are the main features one can expect to find in a Catholic church. Each church has its own character and decor. Some of what was expressed here is not essential, but all expressions are helpful.

Genuflection   *A brief kneeling on the right knee as a sign of respect before the Blessed Sacrament*

Lectionary   *The book of Scripture readings used at Mass*

Sacrarium   *Special sink for washing the sacred vessels used at Mass*

Sacristy   *A room for the storage of sacred vessels, vestments, and so forth, in a church; sometimes used for vesting*

IV

Why Do Catholics Call Priests "Father"?

**Ministry—Religious—Laity—
Catechumenate—Monastery—
Celibacy—Mendicants—Seminary—
Jesuits—Ordination—Priest—
Novitiate—Diaconate—Divine Office—
Breviary—Contemplative Religious
Community—Active Religious
Community—Habit—Altar Server—
Lector—Eucharistic Minister—
Sacristan—Usher—Catechist—Director
of Religious Education—Parish Council**

Introduction

Suppose Jesus had lived, died, and risen from the dead
. . . and nobody noticed. Suppose Jesus had come to earth
as a self-sufficient, solitary prophet. Jesus saw the
importance of gathering the community of apostles around

him. The apostles and disciples shared, helped, and supported Jesus in his mission. As St. Paul said to the Romans:

> *"How then are they to call on him if they have not come to believe in him? And how can they believe in him if they have never heard of him? And how will they hear of him unless there is a preacher for them? And how will there be preachers if they are not sent? As scripture says:* How beautiful are the feet of the messenger of good news. *But it is in that way faith comes, from hearing, and that means hearing the word of Christ."*—Romans 10:14–15,17

Jesus knew that the apostles and those following the apostles would have to speak his words. Through these words, comes our faith.

Throughout the years, many others have shared the work which Christ began: spreading the Good News. The very existence of the Church depends on dedicated persons to carry on the teachings and love of Christ.

In this chapter, we will explore the roles of service the Church utilizes to continue its mission. We begin by explaining the term **ministry,** which in recent years has taken on a variety of meanings. In a brief overview, we look at the historical and social conditions that affected types of service to the Church over the years. We then proceed to consider the distinct roles of priest, **religious,** and laity in the light of recent changes, with special attention to the new opportunities for ministry which have sprung up since Vatican II.

Minister and Ministry

Since the renewal efforts of Vatican II, words have come into our Catholic vocabulary which have taken on a variety of meanings. Two words which need further clarification are *minister* and *ministry.* The dictionary defines a *minister* as "one who serves another," and *ministry* refers to the "type of service given."

These words can be used in several contexts. We speak of a Minister of Foreign Affairs. In the political realm, ministry refers to an agency which serves the people. Protestant clergy are usually called ministers and their role of service, the ministry.

Ministry *Service in or to the Church*

Religious *A man or woman, men or women, who belong to a religious community and make vows*

Since Vatican II, these terms have entered Catholic vocabulary and refer to any type of service one does for the Church. We speak of Eucharistic ministers, pastoral ministers, and ministry to the sick. In the broadest sense, *minister* has come to mean anyone who serves another in the name of Christ. Even the one who greets has been called a minister of hospitality.

This extension of meaning has caused some confusion and discussion. There are those who feel the terms *minister* and *ministry* ought to apply only to one who is ordained. Others contend that the broad sense (that is, use of the words for all types of service) is appropriate, since they all minister in the name of Christ. Vatican II, in the documents, refers to *apostolate* when speaking of roles of service. However, since these words have come into general usage, while we realize the theological nuances involved, minister and ministry are used for the various forms of parish service and work for the Church.

Historical Overview of Service Roles in the Church

The early Christian community was so bound in love with each other that many lived a common lifestyle, and in 1 Peter we read: "put your gifts at the service of one another." (1 Peter 4:10) The Acts of the Apostles relates how the early Christians built up the Body of Christ.

Gradually, leaders emerged, possibly those at whose home the faithful gathered for prayer. These elders who presided at the worship soon came to be known as *epicopoi* and *presbyteroi*—Greek words meaning "leader" and "elder." We derive our words *bishop* and *priest* from these terms.

Later, deacons were appointed to tend to the temporal needs of the community. The community shared in the mission of Christ in a variety of roles.

After the persecutions, the intimacy of the early Christian community gave way to formal structures. Those who wished to become Christian underwent a thorough preparation called the **catechumenate.** Although they were accepted by the community, the bishop presided.

Catechumenate *Period of preparation for the baptism of adults, sometimes of children*

So it seems that in the early days of Christianity, the bishop led the assembly. Later, the service of bishop and priest took on a full-time position.

There were some who responded to the admonition of Christ, "Go and sell what you have . . . come and follow me." (Mark 10:21) These who desired to lead a more intense life of prayer sometimes became hermits and lived alone. Others who followed their example became known as **monks,** since they lived in the community. When many monks joined together, the places they lived in were called **monasteries.**

By the fifth century, the monk became recognized as the ideal, and bishops were chosen from among them. Thus **celibacy,** which the monks professed, became a respected and accepted tradition. Celibacy did not become the rule until the twelfth century, although there were still some exceptions. People were drawn to the monks because of their piety and learning. Towns were built around the monastery and the laity looked to the monks for spiritual guidance. When the feudal system was established, the work of the Church was carried on by the monks together with the nobles. The nobility provided church buildings and the peasants were ministered unto.

The dichotomy between the clergy and laity continued to grow. To participate in a Crusade to try to recapture the Holy Land became a heroic deed, and peasants, as well as clergy and popes, joined the endeavor.

Francis of Assisi saw a need for ministering to the ordinary lay person. He preached a simple Christianity, one to which the peasants could relate. The mysteries of faith were seen in their human dimension, and several devotions and prayers centered around the birth of Christ and his sufferings.

Celibacy   *The chosen unmarried state of life required of priests in the Roman Catholic Church*

Francis of Assisi   *A saint from Italy who lived 1182–1226, founder of the Franciscan mendicant order*

Monastery   *The dwelling place for a community of monks or nuns*

Monk   *A religious priest or brother of a monastic order, usually living in a monastery*

Saint Dominic, around the same time, preached and taught the laity. He popularized the rosary and devotion to Mary. Dominicans also became important teachers in universities.

Through these **mendicants** and their teaching, the laity felt they shared in the work of the Church. However, in official worship the laity still retained their passivity. Although there was a rebirth of learning and culture through the Renaissance, service to the Church was reserved for the monks who copied the sacred manuscripts and the nobles who became the clergy.

Abuses and contradictions led to the Reformation, which sought to correct errors. The Church eventually reacted to the Reformation with the Council of Trent. The Church assumed a defensive stance and sought to rid the Church of abuses.

To provide adequate formation and education of the clergy, **Saint Charles Borromeo** established separate institutions called **seminaries.** They were under the tutelage of the local bishop. This system gave rise to the diocesan priest or secular priest.

Another way the Church sought to insure itself against abuses and false beliefs and to be a more visible sign to the people was through temporal works of charity.

Religious congregations were founded to minister to the spiritual and temporal needs of the times. **Saint Ignatius of Loyola** founded the **Jesuits** who, as teachers and missionaries, worked throughout the world. Hospitals, schools, and other institutions were operated by other active religious communities.

Jesuits   *Society of Jesus, a religious order of men founded in 1534 by Saint Ignatius of Loyola*

Mendicants   *Religious orders without property rights whose members worked or begged for their support*

Saint Charles Borromeo   *Sixteenth century cardinal and saint who actively promoted the education of the clergy*

Saint Dominic   *Saint of the thirteenth century, founder of the Dominican mendicant order*

Saint Ignatius of Loyola   *Sixteenth century saint, founder of the Society of Jesus (Jesuits), author of* The Book of Spiritual Exercises

Seminary   *A house of study and formation in preparation for the priesthood*

The Church still continued to emphasize a legalistic and defensive role. The security and safeguard against error rested in the laws of the Church. This attitude served a purpose for the time of the Reformation. However, it lasted for four hundred years. To be a good Catholic meant that one obeyed the laws of the Church and did good works.

The renewal of Vatican II drastically changed the situation and allowed different forms of service to emerge. The laity's role was recognized as vital to the well-being of the Church. All are called to holiness, and, therefore, the laity also share in the mission of Christ in an active way. One of the main concerns Vatican II aimed to address was the laity's fuller participation in the witness and worship of the Church.

Although the roles of clergy and laity remain distinct, Vatican II looks at each from a different perspective. In this manner, the spirit of the first Christians thrives today. Commitment to the person and work of Christ through shared ministry, pastoral concerns, lay involvement, and teamwork have been introduced into Catholic ministries in the spirit of renewal.

Contemporary needs of the modern age require that the Church respond accordingly. Therefore, the roles of service which have emerged attempt to bring the Catholic faith to the world in meaningful expressions through a variety of ministries.

The Ordained Ministry— Priesthood

The Second Vatican Council asserts that the whole People of God share in the priesthood of Christ. But the priesthood of ordination differs from the priesthood of baptism in essence and degree. Ordination to the priesthood through the Sacrament of **Holy Orders** sets a man apart to serve as a Catholic **priest.** The ministry of Christ has been handed on from the apostles to the bishops, who in turn

Holy Orders   *The sacrament by which a deacon, priest, or bishop is ordained*

Priest   *A man who is ordained; officiates at liturgy, administers the sacraments, and ministers to people's spiritual needs*

transmit to the priest the spiritual power to celebrate the liturgy, forgive sins, and administer all the other sacraments. A Catholic believes that the priest works and acts in the name of Christ through his **ordination.** When a priest blesses, it is Christ who does so. When he offers Mass, it is in the name of Christ.

There are different kinds of priests. A diocesan or secular priest is directly under the authority of his bishop. A religious or order priest, one who belongs to a religious community, is under the authority of his religious superior and takes religious vows, including poverty, chastity, and obedience.

A man who feels the call to the diocesan priesthood, is accepted by the bishop for seminary training, which focuses on the candidate's personal spiritual formation, as well as theological knowledge. After he completes four years of college and four years of theology, he is accepted for ordination. He first is ordained a deacon and interns in a parish or other ministry before being ordained a priest.

If a man chooses to become a religious priest, like a Jesuit or **Maryknoll** Father, he enters the religious community and goes through a period of preparation, including the **novitiate.** He then professes religious vows before being ordained.

A priest's main role is to provide sacramental and liturgical services. He celebrates the liturgy; presides at the sacraments; preaches and performs other pastoral roles, such as counseling.

All priests, after being ordained into the **diaconate,** are bound to celibacy.

Diaconate   *The first of the major orders of holy orders, received prior to ordination to the priesthood (transitional diaconate) or with the intent to remain a deacon (permanent diaconate)*

Maryknoll   *Catholic Foreign Mission Society of America, a religious order founded in 1911*

Novitiate   *A formal period of trial and formation for a man or woman preparing for membership in a religious community*

Ordination   *Those rites in which there is a laying on of hands that invests the man with official priestly authority*

The priest is not by virtue of ordination endowed with full ecclesial powers. He must be called to orders and accepted for service in ministry by the bishop, who bestows on the priest **faculties,** that is, the right to exercise his priestly office within the diocese.

A priest also participates in the official prayer of the Church by the **Divine Office.** Daily he recites the **Breviary,** which are designated psalms, prayers, and readings. He is unified and bound with all others and the whole Church through his prayer life, which is an outgrowth of the Judaic and monastic traditions.

If, for a serious reason, a priest wishes to be relieved of his priestly duties, he goes through **laicization,** the process by which he is returned to the status of a lay person. He may receive the sacraments, but may not exercise his priesthood, except in the extreme emergency when no other priest is available.

Most priests are involved in parish work. If he is in charge of a parish, the priest is a **pastor.** He can be aided by an assistant or associate pastor. The priest temporarily designated to run the parish is the administrator. A priest is addressed as "Reverend" and is called "Father," a carryover from monastic traditions.

A priest who distinguishes himself by outstanding service may be named a **monsignor.** This is an honorary title and does not carry with it any extra power, except as a mark of respect and precedence at liturgical functions. A monsignor may wear a violet cassock and violet trim at official functions. He is addressed "Very Reverend" or "Right Reverend" (depending on rank) and is called "Monsignor."

Breviary   *The liturgical book containing the Divine Office*

Divine Office   *The public, official, and common prayer of the Church*

Faculties   *The right a priest has to exercise his priestly office within the diocese*

Laicization   *The process by which a priest is returned to the status of a lay person*

Monsignor   *An honorary title given to a priest who distinguishes himself by outstanding service*

Pastor   *An ordained minister charged with responsibility for the people committed to his care, for example, a parish priest or the bishop of a diocese*

Priests may also serve as administrators, missionaries, counselors, canon lawyers, or theologians. A priest may also be a member of a contemplative community as a monk. A priest who serves in an institution, hospital, military base, or prison is a **chaplain.** A priest, religious, or lay person serving the spiritual needs at a college is called a **campus minister.**

A priest who belongs to a religious community is supported by and contributes his salary to the community because he professes the vow of poverty. A diocesan priest retains his salary and stipends and may invest them as he chooses.

Since Vatican II, the role of the priest has become more challenging because of the many changes in the Church. It is his responsibility to implement them and explain what the Church intends. A priest does more than preside at liturgy and administer sacraments. The priest today must be flexible, open, and capable of living with uncertainty and change. He is expected to be a group dynamics expert, counselor, computer analyst, organizer, theologian, and leader. Above all, he must be able to be a true pastor, sensitive to the needs of the people.

This new climate calls for a style of leadership in which collaboration, cooperation, and lay involvement are necessary ingredients. For some, the new way is a welcome change, while others find the adjustment a serious challenge, if not an outright threat. Change calls for constant readjustment.

Another challenge to the priesthood today is the issue of celibacy. Although celibacy has been rooted in Catholic tradition since the monastic age, the issue today is questioned. Since the shortage of priests is felt in many sectors, some believe optional celibacy will solve the problem. Others believe the permission to have married clergy will open Pandora's box to a new set of problems. The debate continues to be controversial.

The dearth of priests is still a reality. Part of the situation has been alleviated by the admission of older men to the priesthood. The increasing number of widowers applying has given rise to seminaries specifically designed for older vocations.

Campus Minister   *A priest, religious, or lay person serving the spiritual needs at a college*

Chaplain   *A priest appointed for the pastoral service of an institution, hospital, division of the military, religious community, or various groups of the faithful*

In recent years, some members of the Protestant clergy who converted to Catholicism have been ordained as Catholic priests. Former Episcopalian priests who have been ordained as Catholic priests have remained married.

While the priesthood, like all aspects of Catholic life, has drastically changed, the vital role the priest plays in Catholic faith will endure.

The Ordained Ministry— The Diaconate

Deacons are first mentioned in the Acts of the Apostles when there was a need to tend to the temporal needs of the Greek-speaking Jewish Christian community. In the sixth chapter of Acts we read:

> *"Choose seven men among you who are known to be full of the Holy Spirit and wisdom and we will put them in charge of this matter. . . .The group presented them to the apostles, who prayed and placed their hands on them." —Acts 6:3,6*

From earliest days, the deacon was considered as one set apart for service. As the Church developed and became structured, the role of deacon, as one who served the temporal needs, diminished. The role of service was eventually taken over completely by the role of preparing for ordination to the priesthood; the diaconate came to be a stepping-stone to the priesthood. This form still exists today in what we call the **transitional diaconate.**

Permanent Diaconate

One of the most significant changes of Vatican II came with the restoration of the **permanent diaconate** in 1967. This office enables men, who may be married, to share more directly in the mission of Christ through service to the Church as deacons. The permanent diaconate is a ministry in its own right and is not to be considered as a stepping-stone to priesthood.

Permanent Diaconate   *The first of the major orders of holy orders*

Transitional Diaconate   *The first of the major orders of holy orders, received prior to ordination to the priesthood*

Any unmarried man who is twenty-five and any married man who is thirty-five is eligible to prepare for the diaconate. After being accepted by the bishop the candidate enters a formation program. Many dioceses have their own program, which includes the study of theology, pastoral ministry, and personal spirituality. Since the candidate usually holds a full-time job outside the ministry, the formation takes place on weekends and requires several nights a week for study and practical experience. The process takes from three to five years before one is ordained as a permanent deacon.

After ordination, the deacon belongs to the clerical state, having received the first level of holy orders. If he is unmarried, he cannot marry after ordination. Appointed by the bishop to serve in a specific ministry, the deacon may preach homilies, distribute Communion, administer baptism, witness at matrimony, proclaim the gospel, and officiate at wakes and funerals. He assists at liturgical functions and can preside at other prayer services, such as Bible vigils, stations of the cross, blessing of throats, distributing of ashes, and the administering of other sacramentals.

A deacon is entitled to wear the priestly vestments: the alb and the stole, which is draped over the left shoulder and fastened at the right side. A permanent deacon does not ordinarily wear the clerical collar, but in some cases, he may do so if his identity as a cleric needs to be more clearly defined, as when he would be acting as a parish administrator.

The permanent deacon is a boon to larger parishes who have a dearth of priests. In smaller parishes, too, the deacon can provide services when a priest is not available. Permanent deacons serve well as marriage counselors and in the marriage preparation sessions. They also are effective in the workplace, for they have access to the world of politics, business, and other civil areas to which other clerics have no contact. A permanent deacon's ministry takes place in hospitals, nursing homes, or in the parish. He may be hired full-time by the Church or may retain his occupation.

Because the ministry is relatively new in our Church today, it brings with it specific challenges. A permanent deacon must also establish priorities. For him, his family, marriage, and job must be considered his prime commitment and vocation. A permanent deacon needs the full support of his wife and family. To assist in this regard, many dioceses have developed programs which include the wives and family.

Although money is not his chief motive, the deacon should be justly compensated. This is balanced by the belief that the deacon has a specific vocation to serve.

Once ordained, the permanent deacon continues his formation with ongoing programs set up by the diocese.

The role of the permanent deacon is particularly strong in the United States, which has about sixty percent of the world's deacons. According to the *Catholic Almanac,* there are 11,733 permanent deacons throughout the world.[1] There are nearly eight thousand permanent deacons in the United States, with several thousand in formation. There is a cry for the service of deacons in the Third World and in other areas where there is a shortage of priests.

The role of permanent deacon is still misunderstood in places. It stems from the deep chasm that existed for centuries between clergy and laity. It is hard to conceive of one's next door neighbor as being a cleric while living a lay lifestyle.

The evolution of the permanent deacon will continue and become a more visible aspect of the Church in due time. There is even discussion of the possibility of women being accepted. No matter what form emerges, the permanent diaconate answers a vital need. Someone aptly defined a permanent deacon as a "minister of charity and service in a business suit." As the permanent deacon becomes a more permanent feature of the contemporary Church, it will become more evident that a family man can indeed be a dedicated man of God. Who knows what changes it will lead to in the future?

Religious Life

Since early Christian times, there have been persons who have dedicated themselves in a special way to the Lord through a life of prayer and work. Religious life, as it has come to be known, has evolved and taken different forms over the years.

Today, there are two main types of religious within the Church: the contemplative and the active. Recognized by the Church and subject to Canon Law, each religious community has been founded for a specific purpose and carries on its work in a unique spirit or charism. Although the basic purpose of all religious communities lies in spreading the mission of Christ, there is great variety in the works and lifestyles of religious.

---

1. Felician Foy, O.F.M., ed. *Catholic Almanac* (Huntington, Indiana: Our Sunday Visitor, 1986), p. 365.

Contemplative Religious Orders

The contemplative life is the earliest form of religious dedication, beginning with the monks who lived in the desert. Persons who are contemplatives live cloistered, that is, in a monastery with minimum contact with the outside world. They profess solemn vows, lead a life of intense prayer, and recite the Divine Office in common. Men contemplatives are monks. Women contemplatives are nuns. Contemplatives are self-supporting. They farm, make Communion wafers, vestments, bread, wine, cheese, and other products. The **Carmelites** and **Trappists** are well-known **contemplative religious communities.**

Active Religious Congregations

Up until the sixteenth century, most religious, except for mendicant orders of men, were contemplatives. In time, the need for specific dedicated ministries became apparent and religious congregations mushroomed. Soon the variety and number of religious engaged in active apostolates spread to wherever the Catholic Church existed. Today there are hundreds of different congregations each with its specific character and concern.

Men who belong to religious congregations can be priests or brothers. Those who are professed but not ordained are brothers. Women religious who engage in the active apostolate are called sisters.

Religious Life Today in the Spirit of Vatican II

The challenge of renewal was taken most seriously by active religious congregations. Many had been founded shortly after the Council of Trent and their lifestyle and ways remained medieval.

Carmelites   *Contemplative religious communities of men and of women*

Contemplative Religious Community   *Religious life lived in secluded monasteries; prayer forms the center of the life and work*

Trappists   *Contemplative religious community of men; Trappistines are the women counterparts*

To update their constitutions, their basic way of life, was the first task undertaken. Religious evaluated their ministry in the light of gospel values and sought to rediscover their specific charism. As a result, new constitutions helped religious respond to the needs of the Church of the twentieth century.

Another area greatly affected by the changes was the ministry of religious. Usually, hospitals, schools, and other institutions were conducted under the auspices of religious communities. Today with the complexity of modern technology, the work of religious involves them more directly with the ministries of service. Although many religious congregations have handed over their large institutions to other professional administrators, the religious who staffed them are concentrating their energies to minister to the needy. In addition to their traditional works, religious today work with the homeless, in prisons, in soup kitchens. They teach and nurse and respond wherever the love of Christ can be shown.

Another area where change is evident is the way religious, especially sisters, dress. For hundreds of years people were used to seeing sisters swathed in yards of serge with starched cumbersome headgear. These **habits** originated at the time many religious communities were founded. Many communities adopted the costumes of the villagers which consisted of starched and coifed bonnets that were elaborate and distinctive. When religious communities spread to other countries, the sisters took their distinctive garb along. So what became the habit in one country was actually the costume of the women in another.

Religious habits became the sign and distinguishing trait of sisters. In updating, many religious communities found the ancient garb difficult to maintain. And so changes in this regard were adopted. Today, each religious community has interpreted its manner of dress as it deems appropriate. Some sisters retain the traditional habit, others have modified it, and others choose to dress in the manner of those to whom they minister, as Mother Teresa wears the sari of the Indian women.

As new forms of ministry emerge and religious lifestyles change, religious communities continue to reevaluate their quality of presence.

The dwindling and aging numbers of religious, due to fewer vocations, present a new challenge to the religious. It may be a critical aspect, but then again, it may be a sign of the times. With the laity becoming more involved with the mission of the Church, religious need to step back and join hands with the laity in cooperation and collaboration.

Religious life, no matter to what form it evolves, will nevertheless be relevant to the Church as a counterculture sign and radical witness of total dedication to Christ through the religious vows.

Before we consider the role of the laity, there is another less obvious dedication that is overlooked and even unknown by many. Some dedicated souls live a dedicated quiet life of charity and prayer while living in the world. These persons who hold a secular job often belong to a third order or a secular institute. They take private vows and benefit spiritually from the fact of belonging to a religious institute. Many active and contemplative communities today have associates, men and women of like mind who share in the spirit of the community and often work closely with members of the community.

Habit *Distinctive clothing of a religious man or woman*

Laity and the Challenge of Vatican II

One of the most serious concerns of Vatican II focused on the call of the laity to bring Christ into the modern world. Since the laity throughout history had been relegated to a passive and receptive stance, the laity needed to be made aware of their significant role and responsibility.

In order that the Church be a viable active presence of Christ, the laity are called to an intense dynamic involvement. The challenge sounded loudly in the "Dogmatic Constitution on the Church": "The obligation of spreading the faith is imposed on every disciple of Christ."[2] All are called by baptism to proclaim the Good News of Christ, and to bring the spiritual dimension into the world.

Vatican II has bestowed on the lay vocation a dignity hitherto ignored. In the "Decree on the Apostolate of Lay People," we read: "Laymen . . . do not separate their union with Christ from their ordinary life; but through the very performance of their tasks, which are God's will for them, they actually promote the growth of their union with him."[3]

The laity, by their unique opportunities, can permeate society and the workplace with Christian values and witness to Christ wherever they live and work. This aspect of total involvement in the world cannot be underplayed. When we speak of the participation of the laity in the work of the Church, we cannot associate it merely to reading the Scriptures or to other Church-related activities.

The laity need to witness to their baptismal commitment. This does not mean wearing one's religion on one's sleeve nor sharing it in preachy self-righteousness. Rather, one is called to integrate one's whole life, the mundane with the holy, into a vibrant spirituality. The laity are called to develop a mature, active, and adult faith which can transform the world. It is a subtle, powerful mode of injecting values into the world. It is compassion to the less fortunate. It is caring for the downtrodden. It is standing up for justice. It is fairness in all one's business dealings.

---

2. Walter M. Abbott, S.J., ed. "Dogmatic Constitution on the Church," *The Documents of Vatican II* (New York: America Press, 1966), p. 36, article 17.
3. Austin Flannery, O.P., ed. "Decree on the Apostolate of Lay People," *Vatican Council II* (Collegeville, Minnesota: The Liturgical Press, 1975), p. 770, article 4.

"Since it is proper to the layman's state of life for him to spend his days in the midst of the world and of secular transactions, he is called by God to burn with the spirit of Christ and to exercise his apostolate in the world as a kind of leaven."[4]

The laity, too, are challenged to become more involved in the work of the Church. New forms of parish ministry have evolved which allow the laity more active participation.

The revised Code of Canon Law affirms: "Qualified lay persons are capable of assuming from their sacred pastors those ecclesiastical offices and functions which they are able to exercise in accord with the prescriptions of law."[5]

Since the laity carry out their baptismal commitment to serve, the parish is where the laity are most involved in Church-related ministries. The opportunities for participation embrace the whole gamut of parish life and work.

Types of Lay Ministry

First, there are the liturgical or Eucharistic ministries. Many parishes have a special liturgical committee which arranges and plans meaningful liturgy celebrations, especially for Sundays and special feasts and observances. The main roles for laity involvement with liturgy itself include:

• **Eucharistic ministers** who are authorized to distribute Communion during Mass and take it to the sick.

• **Lectors** who carry the Lectionary in the Entrance Procession and read the first two readings and responsories at Mass.

---

4. Walter M. Abbott, S.J., ed. "Decree on the Apostolate of the Laity," *The Documents of Vatican II* (New York: America Press, 1966), p. 492, article 2.
5. Canon Law Society of America, *Code of Canon Law* (Washington, D.C.: Canon Law Society of America, 1983), p. 77, c. 228.

Eucharistic Minister   *A person who distributes Communion at Mass or who takes Communion to the homebound or those in hospitals and nursing homes*

Lector   *The person who proclaims the first two Scripture readings at the Sunday Mass or the first reading at a weekday Mass*

• Leaders of song who announce hymns, teach new ones, sing solo parts, and lead the congregational singing. Some parishes also enlist the services of ministers of music who lead the choir and are in charge of the music selections.

• Congregants who present the gifts of bread and wine in the Offertory Procession.

• **Altar servers** assist the priest at Mass, light candles, hold the book, and do other tasks around the altar. They dress either in their best clothes or in a special cassock and surplice.

Surplice

Cassock

There are others whose service is necessary for the liturgy, but they do not take part in the celebration itself. The **sacristan** prepares the vessels and takes care of the altar linens. **Ushers** perform a vital service in showing people to their seats and in taking up the collection. Some parishes have designated certain volunteers as ministers of hospitality, who welcome newcomers and those celebrating at the liturgy, and arrange for refreshments after liturgies.

Altar Servers   *Those who assist the priest at Mass, such as helping to prepare the altar*

Sacristan   *The person who takes care of the sanctuary, sacred vessels, and altar linens*

Ushers   *Ministers of hospitality who usually greet those entering the church, collect the offerings, and direct movement at the time of Communion*

A most vital service is done by the **sexton,** the one who locks and unlocks the church, repairs what breaks down, and acts as overall upkeep manager. This person is often taken for granted, but would be the one you miss if not on the job.

Second, there are the educational and administrative ministries.

• Most parishes now employ a **Director of Religious Education** (DRE) who is qualified in religious studies or theology and directs the religious education programs for children attending public schools, the sacramental programs, adult education, and other educational endeavors.

• **Catechists** teach the religion classes and are commissioned by the pastor. The personnel in the parochial schools, the principal and teachers, who are either lay or religious, also serve in a vital ministry. Many parish schools welcome the services of aides and volunteers in school programs.

• Some parishes have hired youth ministers; pastoral ministers, who visit the sick and homebound; and adult education directors.

• **Parish councils,** made up of representatives of laity along with the clergy, aid the pastor in a team approach to ministry, integrating the activities and overall working of the parish.

• In places where there is no resident clergy, a lay person may be appointed as administrator to control the running of the parish and conduct Communion and prayer services. Visiting priests offer the liturgy and administer the sacraments.

Catechist   *A person who teaches religion in parochial schools, parish religion programs, RCIA, and so forth*

Director of Religious Education   *(DRE) or Coordinator (CRE); person who directs the religious education programs of a parish*

Parish Council   *Representatives of the laity in a parish who assist the pastor and staff in the overall running of the parish*

Sexton   *Infrequently used term for a church maintenance person*

Last, but not least, there are those untitled ministries necessary for the true spirit in a parish. There are, what I call, the "pray-ers," the faithful few who attend daily Mass and live a life of intense prayer. You can count on these dedicated souls for any special intention you may have. There are the "Never-No-Sayers," who are the ones anyone can depend on for anything. Call them to pick up an elderly person for Church, ask them to help with a bake sale, or to lend a hand. They are always ready and willing. There are the "parish missionaries." These people extend an invitation to the lax members and bring them to Church. There are the "silent presences," the mourners at funerals, the ones who send cards to the sick, and in a spirit of caring boost the lonely.

A parish can consider itself blessed which has many untitled ministers. "The harvest is good but laborers are scarce." (Matthew 9:37) Lay involvement in parish work is so diverse, there is room for all.

Today's Implications

Since this active role of the laity is an about-face of previous attitudes, new challenges have arisen. Lay involvement need not blur the distinction between clergy and laity. It is a two-sided endeavor. Laity need to come forward and lend their expertise and talents. Clergy need to accept the assistance without being threatened. Laity, in becoming more involved in Church-related activities, must keep their priorities in perspective and not allow their family life to suffer because of their work at Church.

The new responsibility of laity calls for a mature adult faith, capable of living in the spirit of Vatican II. It requires an informed faith, one that is well-read in recent theological trends, one which is capable of responsible moral decisions. A gap which still cries out for fulfillment is an adult-centered catechesis and serious spiritual formation for adults. The Church has done well in educating the children, but many adults without further formation have remained at the level of childhood faith. Parishes need to address the educational needs for adults.

"Since in our times the women have an ever more active share in the whole life of society, it is very important that they participate more widely also in the various fields of the Church's apostolate."[6]

---

6. Walter M. Abbott, S.J., ed. "Decree on the Apostolate of the Laity," *The Documents of Vatican II* (New York: America Press, 1966), p. 500, article 9.

That is how Vatican II realized the role of women in the Church. Yet, in practical ways, there is continuing debate concerning a more responsible role. The Church has always depended on its women, but in service and subsidiary positions. What would parishes be without women? They have taught in the schools, played the organ, cleaned the church, kept parish records. As long as women are excluded from leadership and administrative roles, as long as there exists a patriarchal dominance, the debate will continue.

Women's desire to participate more fully does not necessarily mean all women seek ordination, but that they need to be recognized in their own right as equally capable. The issue cannot be resolved by force. It is becoming increasingly evident that when the need becomes crucial for more involvement in ministry, many compassionate, dedicated women will answer the cry. Until then, one wonders how much work of the Church remains undone.

As the Church becomes more aware of the needs of the times, opportunities for ministries will multiply, and hopefully, the Church will tap all of its resources. Issues of contemporary vital concerns cannot be ignored. The ministry to divorced and separated Catholics, the homeless, abused children, drug addicts, alcoholics, and homosexuals open the way for creative challenges.

The Church is called on to minister to all God's people and be a healing presence, and maybe even a miracle worker. The challenges call for a strong commitment of all who serve in the Church. Priests, religious, and laity need to join hands, reaching out together in cooperation and love to be a catalyst of Christ's continuing presence through healing, teaching, and caring. Whether you call it service, ministry, witness, apostolate, or mission, the work of Christ goes on by the dedicated clergy, religious, and laity who serve the Church.

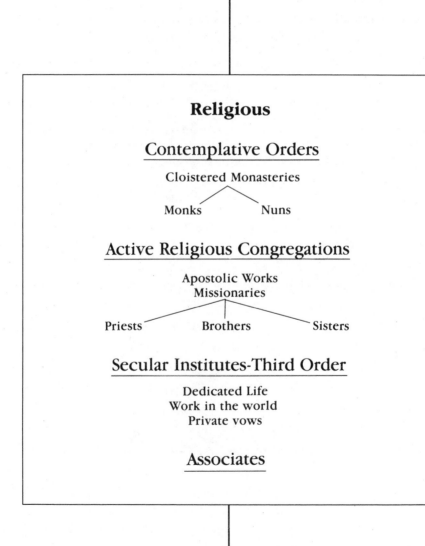

Ministries of Service in the Catholic Church

Religious

Contemplative Orders

Cloistered Monasteries

Monks   Nuns

Active Religious Congregations

Apostolic Works
Missionaries

Priests   Brothers   Sisters

Secular Institutes-Third Order

Dedicated Life
Work in the world
Private vows

Associates

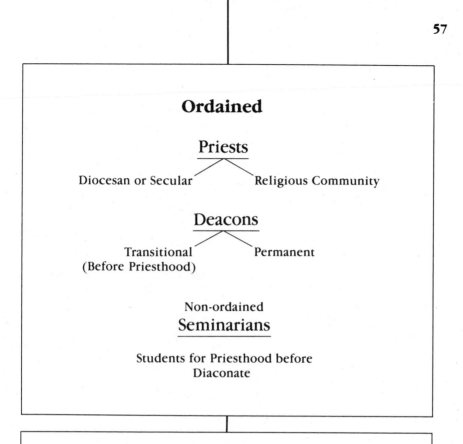

Ordained

Priests

Diocesan or Secular — Religious Community

Deacons

Transitional — Permanent
(Before Priesthood)

Non-ordained
Seminarians

Students for Priesthood before
Diaconate

Laity

Liturgical Roles	Educational— Administrative	Social Outreach
• Eucharistic Minister	• Director of Religious Education (DRE)	• Pastoral Minister
• Lector	• Principal–Teacher	• Parish Organizations
• Cantor-Music Minister	• Catechist	• Support Groups
• Altar Server-Acolyte	• Parish Council	• Special Concerns Committees
• Usher	• Parish Administrator	
• Sacristan		
• Sexton		
• Greeter		

V

Why Do Catholics Go to Mass?

Mass—Liturgy—Seder Meal—Last Supper—Eucharist—Miracle Play—Tridentine Mass—Vernacular—Sign of Peace—Paschal Mystery—Holy Days of Obligation—Chalice—Paten—Host—Ciborium—Cruets—Corporal—Sacramentary—Vestments—Concelebration

Introduction

Ever since people have recognized that there are powers and forces greater than themselves, they have reached out in efforts to communicate with the gods. People have acted out their inner feelings in human rituals which became sacred when directed to the Divine. From the earliest days of Christianity, believers have gathered together to worship God in the way Jesus directed, "Do this as a remembrance of me." (Luke 22:19)

For Catholics, going to Mass has become the way we worship. Although attending Mass distinguishes a practicing Catholic, this ritual is not merely a weekly obligation; the Mass is the most intense way a Catholic acts out his or her commitment to Christ. The Mass, for Catholics, is the core of the faith around which all other beliefs revolve.

In order to understand the implication of what the Mass means for Catholics after Vatican II, we need to backtrack to its origins and consider the changes and evolution of the Mass through the ages. In this chapter, we consider the original setting which gave rise to our liturgy, the historical situations which affected the mode of worship, and the theological understanding of the Mass. We examine some of the basic externals connected with a worship service and conclude with a practical reflection on how to make one's participation more meaningful.

Original Setting— The Last Supper Remembered

In order to be more aware of what happens at every liturgy, we need to put ourselves into the feelings and emotions of the small band of disciples after Jesus was buried. Like any family who gathers after the death of a loved one, the disciples came together heartbroken, sad, and traumatized by the events of that first Good Friday. Their grief was short-lived. Many of Jesus' friends experienced his presence after the resurrection.

Jesus made a radical difference in every life he touched. He was not gone; they knew he was present in a powerful, different way. They opened up to each other, relating events that they remembered in an effort to engrave his earthly life in their hearts. They recalled words Jesus spoke, miracles he worked, and teachings he imparted. In spirit, they relived every moment. As they reminisced, they probed deeper, shared their impressions and contemplated the meaning of it all.

Through a common religious experience on Pentecost, they were filled with the Spirit and realized beyond a doubt that Jesus truly was the Messiah. Every gesture of that last time together, the **Seder Meal** of Holy Thursday, took on a new dimension. They saw now how that Last Supper, death, and resurrection of Jesus were united in Jesus' supreme messianic role.

Seder Meal   *Jewish feast celebrated in the home with a meal; commemorates the exodus of the Israelites from Egypt; part of the Passover celebration*

They recalled how Jesus took bread and wine, blessed it, and gave it to them saying: "Take this and eat it . . . this is my body." (Matthew 26:26) And saying: "Do this as a remembrance of me." (Luke 22:19) These words took on new meaning.

Each Sunday these faithful disciples gathered. They celebrated the resurrection, recalled Jesus' life, and shared a meal in remembrance of Jesus. Jesus' presence lived on in their lives. These gatherings in faith have continued to this day. It is the "New Covenant," the **"Eucharist"** (thanksgiving), the "liturgy" (work of the people), and the "Missa" (Mass), a strengthening for one's mission in life.

The small intimate gathering of the disciples has evolved into a complex ritual through the years. It is impossible to consider what the Mass means for Catholics today without tracing, in broad outlines, the development and various understandings of the Mass. In our renewal efforts to recapture the spirit of the early Church, we need to explore how the liturgy has been interpreted and changed according to circumstances.

Development of the Liturgy

The early Jewish believers soon came to realize that their worship of God was complete through the Lord's Supper, which they celebrated in light of the resurrection. And so they observed Sunday as the Lord's Day, while incorporating elements of their Jewish heritage into the Eucharist. Soon Gentiles joined, and spontaneous rituals were added as needs arose.

As the believing community increased in size, the worship was no longer connected with a meal. The Lord's Supper became a service, with a less spontaneous format. After the Edict of Milan in 313, when Christians were free to practice their religion publicly, they worshipped in large assembly halls called basilicas.

Greater reforms occurred during the reign of Pope Gregory the Great (590–604). The liturgy became a spectacle and was fashioned on ceremonies borrowed from the Roman court protocol. Latin became its official language. The gestures of bowing, kneeling, and genuflecting added a regal tone. Elaborate music, which came to be

Eucharist   *1. The liturgy of the Mass; 2. Communion or the Sacrament of (Communion); 3. The consecrated bread and wine; 4. Thanksgiving*

known as **Gregorian Chant,** was led by professional choirs. The priest wore the formal Roman garments of court officials, the custom of which was carried over after the fall of the Roman Empire, even up until our present day. Gregorian reforms continued to influence the Church in all places where the Church became established.

In feudal times, the nobles erected the churches, and often the liturgy was celebrated in their private chapels. The Mass soon became the personal worship of the priest, while the people were permitted to be onlookers. The people no longer brought gifts to share, but they still wished to benefit from the spiritual graces of the Mass. To guarantee a part in the blessing, the laity offered sums of money so that the celebrant would pray for their intentions. Thus began the custom of **stipends.**

Abuses crept in and resulted in the buying and selling of spiritual favors. This sin of **simony** was condemned by the Council of Trent. However, the stipend contributes to the support of the priest and is not intended to pay for a Mass.

In the Middle Ages, the Mass isolated the laity even more. The Mass was said in Latin, which no one understood. The priest was far removed with his back to the people. The people tired of being mere spectators, and so they started acting out the gospel stories as a tableau while the Mass was said. These **miracle plays** continued for years. To alert the laity at the consecration, bells were rung, so the people could offer adoration to the **Real Presence.** The Eucharist was to be adored, and the laity refrained from receiving Communion. They prayed private prayers. Liturgy belonged to the priest. False beliefs started circulating about what went on at the altar. To forestall rumors, the priest elevated the Sacred Host for the people to see and adore.

Gregorian Chant   *Church music dating back to the sixth century; one-voice, vocal plainsong—sung without organ*

Miracle Play   *Medieval religious dramas meant as teaching aids; preceded morality plays*

Real Presence   *Jesus, true God and true man, really and substantially present, in a mysterious way, under the appearances of bread and wine*

Simony   *Buying and selling spiritual goods*

Stipend   *Monetary offering made to a priest when requesting that a Mass be said for a particular intention or person*

The decadence and lack of true theology led the Council of Trent to attempt to safeguard the truth. Every gesture, ceremony, and ritual was regulated. The **Tridentine Mass,** the liturgy set up by the Council of Trent, aimed at total uniformity. The Mass became the same no matter where it was celebrated. The Mass in a thatched roof chapel in Samoa was identical with a Mass said in Saint Peter's in Rome.

The Mass became standardized, but no more meaningful, because the people did not understand what the Mass really meant. It was something "to go to" in order to be in good standing. This situation lasted for four hundred years until Vatican II began a reform of the liturgy.

Liturgical Reforms of Vatican II

Although there had been previous attempts to reform the liturgy, none were as far-reaching as Vatican II. The task was immense. Where to begin was an issue not easily resolved. But after prayer and reflection, the Church initiated changes which gradually reached the grass roots level.

The basic changes needed to be external in order to bridge the gap between the priest and people. The laity needed to see and experience a more active role. The Mass, in order to be understood, must be in the language of the people, so the **vernacular** soon was introduced. To effect a feeling of intimacy, the altar was moved to face the people and the **communion rail,** which had separated the sanctuary from the nave, was eliminated. Churches built after the renewal, are usually designed so that the altar is in or closer to the middle and emulates the gathering around the table of the Lord.

Gestures assume a symbolic meaning. We stand as a sign of reverence at the Entrance, Gospel, and Lord's Prayer. Kneeling as a sign of submission is no longer a universally meaningful symbol. And so kneeling during the liturgy is minimal, at the consecration.

Communion Rail *A previously used kneeler between the sanctuary and nave of a church*

Tridentine Mass *The Eucharistic liturgy set up by the Council of Trent in the sixteenth century*

Vernacular *The ordinary language of the people*

Even the gestures of the priest, whether regulated or optional, express deeper meanings. Hands extended wide at the Lord's Prayer embrace all who are remembered and in need of prayers; hands folded show a respectful dependence on God.

The laity affirm their faith many times during the liturgy by saying "Amen." This also brings to mind the fact that the sacrifice belongs to the priest and the people. The people, in extending a **sign of peace** to each other, are reminded that, at the Mass, they are a community of believers joined in prayer and love. The handshake serves as a sign of reconciliation.

The option of taking Communion in the hand, a practice some Catholics find difficult, has been introduced to more meaningfully express our openness and dependence on God. To open the hand to receive the Body of Christ shows a willingness to take Jesus into one's heart and then from there out to the world. Many people hesitate to utilize this option because of previous training which forbade one to touch the Sacred Host.

These external changes effect little if one cannot grasp the theological meanings intended. Although the changes aimed at greater lay participation and involvement, Vatican II sought to focus on the true nature of the liturgy and to capture the spirit and fervor of the first Christians. The various theological concepts need to be balanced into a meaningful liturgical celebration.

The liturgy capsulizes a Catholic's faith in Jesus. The Mass recalls Jesus' saving acts through his life, death, and resurrection. It is the entire **Paschal Mystery** brought to reality in a sacramental way. The Eucharist makes Christ present once again, no less powerful than he was to the early Christians assembled in prayer. Jesus is not only remembered but present in a unique sacramental manner under the appearances of bread and wine.

We believe that, of ourselves, we have little of worth to offer God. The offering of Jesus to the Father in the Mass is the perfect gift of love to God. Jesus renews, in a bloodless way, his sacrificial death on the cross.

By sharing in the Eucharist, a Catholic commits himself or herself to what Jesus calls us to—making Jesus present in the world. All one's actions become united with the Lord. We die to self so that we can rise with Christ.

Paschal Mystery   *The passion, death, resurrection, and ascension of Christ*

Sign of Peace   *A greeting to those around one during the Communion Rite of the Mass*

In the Eucharist, we join with other believers to share the presence of the Lord. Together in worship as a community of faith, Catholics witness to the work of Christ in the world.

The Eucharist pulls together one's whole faith experience of the Lord. In his life, in the early Church, in our Churches today, Jesus continues his constant presence through the action of the priest in consecrating the bread and wine. Vatican II challenges Catholics to consider the Mass in its deepest theological dimensions as a precious heritage, the sacramental presence of the Lord in word, sacrament, priest, and people. The Mass is Jesus living on.

Some Practical Considerations about the Liturgy

The congregation usually gathers for Mass in a church. But auditoriums, arenas, homes, or the outdoors are appropriate settings for Mass. Anyone is welcome to attend a Catholic liturgy, but ordinarily only Catholics receive Communion. Mass is celebrated each day. However, this practice has been common only in the last several hundred years. Before that, the liturgy was celebrated only on Sundays and holy days.

Since the Mass is the focal point of faith, a Catholic is expected to attend Mass as an expression of belief. Catholics are bound by Church law to attend Mass on the Lord's Day, either Saturday evening or Sunday, and on the six **holy days of obligation.** Many consider this law an onerous duty. But the law itself was really enacted as a permission and privilege extended to laity; in the Middle Ages, many considered themselves too unworthy to go to Mass and prayed their private devotions instead.

Masses can last from twenty minutes to over an hour, depending on the feast and occasion. Ordinarily a Sunday liturgy is more solemn

Holy Days of Obligation *Days on which Catholics are required to participate in the celebration of Mass; in addition to Sundays, there are six in the United States: Christmas, the Solemnity of Mary (January 1), Ascension (forty days after Easter), Assumption of Mary (August 15), All Saints (November 1), and Immaculate Conception (December 8)*

than the weekday Mass. Pomp and splendor are added on more solemn feasts, as at the Christmas Midnight Mass, with acolytes, incense, processions, and music. These features are meant to enhance the worship and not to distract from it.

Weekday Masses usually are simple and quiet with only a few parishioners present. At least one other person must be in attendance besides the priest in order to celebrate Mass. Mass is a communal celebration, not the priest's personal devotion.

External Preparations for Mass

Usually the vessels to be used in the liturgy are placed on a small table in the aisle and are brought to the priest during the Presentation of the Gifts. The **chalice** or cup, which must be made of durable noncorrodible material, is the most important vessel. During Mass, the wine in it will be changed into the sacramental Blood of Christ. Each priest usually has his own chalice. A small flat dish called a **paten** holds the large **host** which the priest uses at Mass. This host is larger than the ones received by the congregation because it is easier to see when it is elevated at the consecration. In a cup-like vessel called the **ciborium** are the quarter-sized hosts for the people's Communion. These wafers are usually made by pouring batter, made with flour and water, onto waffle irons inscribed with liturgical symbols. The thin flat sheets are cut out as hosts.

Cruets filled with water and wine are also brought up at the Presentation of Gifts. The altar is covered with a white linen cloth which drapes down the sides or covers the altar like a tablecloth. At least two beeswax candles burn near the altar during Mass. A crucifix, on the altar, on a stand, or suspended on the wall, reminds us that the Mass reenacts the Paschal Mystery.

Chalice   *Cup used to hold wine during Mass*

Ciborium   *Cup-like vessel used to hold hosts at Mass*

Cruets   *Small pitchers to hold wine and water at Mass*

Host   *Bread used at Mass*

Paten   *Flat dish to hold the large host (bread) at Mass*

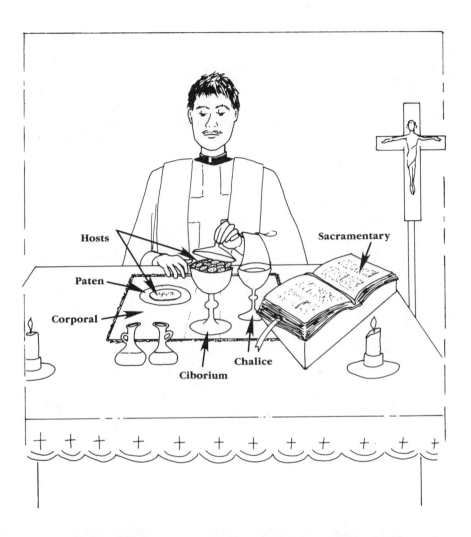

A white cloth about nine inches square, the **corporal,** is spread in the center of the altar. The chalice and ciborium are placed on it during Mass. A small bowl and finger towel, which the priest uses to wash his hands, are also on the altar or on a table nearby.

Corporal   *Square linen cloth placed on altar under chalice and ciborium at Mass*

The **Sacramentary** is placed on the altar and contains the prayers the priest says during Mass. The Lectionary, carried in procession by the lector, contains the Scripture readings. It is placed on the **lectern** from which the Word of God is proclaimed. **Hymnals** and missalettes which contain the hymns and Mass prayers are usually provided for the congregation. The priest consults an **Ordo** which directs him, depending on what feast is observed. He also consults the Mass intention book to know for whom the Mass will be offered.

Hymnal   *Book of hymns used in church*

Lectern   *The reading stand used in church*

Ordo   *Book of directions for the Mass and Divine Office on a daily basis*

Sacramentary   *The book used by the priest which contains the order of Mass*

Since ancient days, the priest has worn vestments derived from the Romans as the distinguishing garb for Mass. An **alb** is a long loose garment reaching to the floor. The **stole,** the symbol of the priesthood, is draped around his neck. The **chasuble,** which means "little house," is a flowing colored outer garment. Its style and color vary with the seasons.

The priest who presides at liturgy is the **celebrant.** If more than one priest celebrates, the Mass is **concelebrated** and the priests are **concelebrants.** When a bishop officiates at a formal Mass, it is an Episcopal Mass. When the pope presides, it is a **Papal Mass.** These externals help us understand better what the Mass means. They also aid us in greater devotion.

Practical Ways to Make the Mass Meaningful

Mass is our communal coming together to worship the Lord. It is helpful, as you enter the church, to do so in a spirit of devotion. "I'm here to give my praise to God. So also are all my fellow worshippers. We come with our own burdens and concerns."

Alb *Long, loose white robe with full sleeves worn under the chasuble by the priest and deacon at Mass*

Celebrant *The priest celebrating a Mass*

Chasuble *Flowing outer garment worn by the priest at Mass*

Concelebrants *The priests celebrating a Mass together*

Concelebration *The simultaneous celebration of Mass by more than one priest, consecrating the same bread and wine*

Papal Mass *A Eucharistic celebration at which the pope presides*

Stole *Long, narrow strip of cloth; vestment, worn across the shoulders and down the front, by the priest; across one shoulder and attached at the waist on the other side, by the deacon*

Unite in prayer with those gathered. There are usually a few moments before the service begins. Many use this time to pray for their own intentions, but also for those of others. As you see people come in, pray for each one. You may know a person needs special help. Join your prayers with theirs, offer spiritual aid. Everyone comes with his or her own agenda. You may take time to read the Scripture readings from the missalette or some reflective passage.

We do not come to Mass "to get something out of it." At Mass, we offer to God the perfect gift, Jesus. The Mass will take its full effect if we approach it not in the coercion of duty, but as a privilege and personal invitation.

At times, the Mass may seem less than perfect. We may be distracted by the music. The mannerisms of the celebrant may grate on our nerves. It may be too stuffy or too drafty. Noisy, crying babies and inconsiderate snifflers may be among the congregants. We are there to praise God, and maybe we need to offer up some petty annoyances as well. The Mass has human elements. Whenever human endeavors are at stake, there is room for improvement. One cannot be guaranteed of a flawless liturgy. It continues to be a sincere human attempt to give praise to God and carry on Christ's mission.

Structure and Format of the Mass

Introductory Rites

We enter the house of the Lord in praise—Entrance Procession

We approach the Lord in humility—Penitential Rite

We praise the Lord—Glory to God in the highest

Liturgy of the Word

We listen to the Word of God—Scripture Readings

We respond to the Word in faith—Responsorial Psalm

We hear the Good News proclaimed—Gospel

We are encouraged to lead a Christian life—Homily

We profess our beliefs—Creed

We pray for the needs of all peoples—General Intercessions

Liturgy of the Eucharist

We bring and offer our gifts—Presentation of the Gifts, Prayer over the Gifts

We praise the Lord—"Holy, Holy. . . ,"—Eucharistic Prayer

We welcome Jesus in his sacramental Presence—Consecration

We remember our loved ones, living and dead

We affirm our faith—"Amen"

We proclaim the mystery of faith and unite in prayer—The Lord's Prayer

We extend the peace of Christ to fellow believers—Sign of Peace

We express our unworthiness and beg for peace—"Lamb of God . . ."

We receive Jesus in the Eucharist and give thanks—Communion

Concluding Rite

We receive the final blessing—that the Spirit be with us

We are challenged to live the Mass—"Go in peace to love and serve the Lord."

We respond generously—"Thanks be to God."

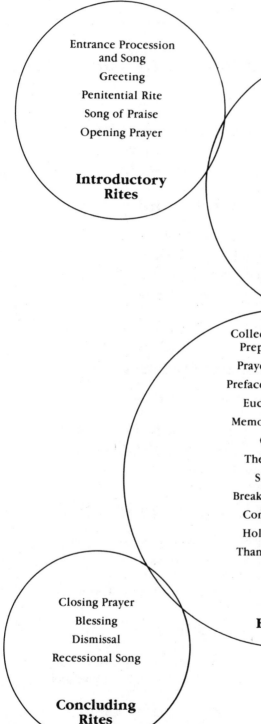

Introductory Rites

Entrance Procession and Song

Greeting

Penitential Rite

Song of Praise

Opening Prayer

Liturgy of the Word

First Reading

Responsorial Psalm

Second Reading

Alleluia Verse

Gospel

Homily

Profession of Faith

General Intercessions

Liturgy of the Eucharist

Collection of Gifts and Preparation of Altar

Prayer over the Gifts

Preface and Acclamation

Eucharistic Prayer

Memorial Acclamation

Great Amen

The Lord's Prayer

Sign of Peace

Breaking of the Bread

Communion Song

Holy Communion

Thanksgiving Prayer

Concluding Rites

Closing Prayer

Blessing

Dismissal

Recessional Song

VI

Why Do Catholics Have Seven Sacraments?

Grace—Baptism—Rite of Christian Initiation of Adults—Limbo—Confirmation—Pentecost—Holy Spirit—Eucharist—Holy Orders—Matrimony—Nuptial Mass—Annulment—Divorce—Reconciliation—Lent—Anointing of the Sick—Viaticum

Introduction

There is something deep within our human psyche which enables us to capture a special moment and keep it alive. We have wedding customs, birthday parties, and retirement send-offs. We preserve memories and allow some of their reality to continue to affect our lives. Signs and symbols reveal deeper meanings. Rings, souvenirs, and mementos are simple things made special.

The early Christian community kept alive the presence of Jesus in special ways. Through sacred rituals, they continued to convey Jesus' actions. He had been with them for so many meals, and the Last Supper especially had come to mean so much. He forgave sin and healed the sick. Jesus promised the apostles they would receive the Spirit to empower them, as they continued his mission and baptized, preached, and spread the Good News in Jesus' name. The bond of love between man and woman was held sacred, for Jesus worked his first miracle at a wedding in **Cana.** This "keeping alive of the saving acts of Jesus" was continued in the early Church, and, although the externals may have changed, the sacraments continue to be essential ways of continuing Christ's mission.

In this chapter, we examine the nature of a sacrament, how the forms have evolved over the years, and offer a brief description of the current theology of each of the seven sacraments: baptism, confirmation, Eucharist, reconciliation, anointing of the sick, holy orders, and matrimony.

Nature of a Sacrament

Catholics have been taught that a sacrament is "an outward sign instituted by Christ to give **grace.**"[1] While this definition is theologically accurate, Vatican II looked at sacraments from a different perspective, giving them a fuller dimension. The sacraments are God's saving acts continued in time. And so, Jesus is the Sacrament of God and the Church is a Sacrament of Jesus. The seven sacraments continue Jesus' mission through the Church.

A sacrament does not dole out some mysterious substance which can be measured. A sacrament is not something given; it is a relationship enriched. Catholics today need to see the sacraments as binding us intimately to Christ who comes to us in life's special moments.

Did we throw out the concept of grace? By no means. But grace today is seen as that relationship which we have with God. And the sacraments become signs to show Christ is acting and relating to us in

---

1. Confraternity of Christian Doctrine, *The New Saint Joseph Baltimore Catechism* (New York: Catholic Book Publishing, 1964), p. 113.

Cana   *The site of Jesus' first miracle when he changed water into wine at a wedding feast*

Grace   *God's life in a person; a free gift*

a special way, at special times, in special needs. As followers of Christ, we are empowered to share his own spiritual life. The sacraments draw us into Jesus' life.

When Catholics make use of the sacraments, God is given honor and worship, and the person is aided toward salvation. Basically, the sacraments are direct ways believers can reach out and touch the Divine, who reaches out to befriend people.

Evolution and Development of the Sacraments

Each sacrament, though not directly mentioned by name in the New Testament, can be traced in tradition to the actions of Jesus and the early Church. Initiation, healing, forgiveness, and leadership all had a sacred character. A variety of rituals developed concerning the way the Church handed on Jesus' spirit.

Since the early Church was fairly unstructured, some Churches ritualized more acts than others. There was a time when there were thirty or forty sacred actions and ritual signs.

The Church spread and the "signs" multiplied. The Fourth Lateran Council in 1215 pronounced that there were seven sacraments.

Theology in the Middle Ages, with its piety and the development of Canon Law, affected sacramental life. Because there came to be restrictions and rules, the faithful looked at the sacraments as some kind of sacred depository. Fulfill certain conditions, and something spiritual would be given—grace.

By the time of the Reformation, excesses and superstitions had crept in. The Council of Trent defined and legislated each sacrament as to its matter and form. Emphasis on correct wording, distinct ritual actions, and the personal state of the soul conveyed an impersonal, legalistic, and cold tone.

It is clear that Vatican II had much overhauling to do. To provide a meaningful renewal of sacramental theology became one of its prime concerns.

Sacraments of Initiation

Baptism, confirmation, and the Eucharist are called the **Sacraments of Initiation** because they were the ways a convert was admitted into the Christian community in the early days, and they were celebrated in one ceremony. Although these sacraments are distinct today and given at separate times, they still are given to adult catechumens in one ceremony: the **Rite of Christian Initiation of Adults.** These sacraments incorporate one into the community of believers and celebrate one's commitment.

Baptism

Through baptism, one is admitted into the Christian community. It was not a ritual thought up by the early Church. The ritual of initiation by water is an ancient one used in many religions, because water is a universal symbol of purification.

Baptism was stipulated by Christ himself: "Go, therefore, and make disciples of all the nations. Baptize them in the name 'of the Father, and of the Son, and of the Holy Spirit.' " (Matthew 28:19)

So, in the early Church, anyone who pledged faith in Christ was baptized. Gradually, in order to guarantee one's sincerity, the adult went through a thorough preparation called the catechumenate. After instruction and prayer and a process of conversion through Rites of Initiation, one was admitted fully into the Christian community. This was done in a solemn manner at the Easter Vigil.

As numbers of converts increased, this method gave way to a singular baptism ceremony in which whole households were admitted into the Christian community. Infant baptism became a common practice in the Church when entire families joined, and also when theological explanations about the necessity of baptism for salvation were emphasized.

Rite of Christian Initiation of Adults *The process (stages and rites) by which unbaptized adults are initiated into the Catholic Church*

Sacraments of Initiation *Baptism, confirmation, and Eucharist; the sacraments by which a person is initiated into the Catholic Church*

Saint Augustine believed that people must be rescued from the sinful state in which they are born, a state he called *original sin*. The concept of commitment to Christ and initiation was overshadowed by the original sin theory which pervaded Catholic theology.

In the Middle Ages, the question was raised concerning the necessity of baptism and the fate of infants who died without baptism. Would God allow an innocent baby to suffer eternally? The answer provided—**limbo**—was satisfactory: Those infants who died without baptism enjoy a natural happiness in a sort of antechamber to heaven, limbo.

This thinking concerning baptism and limbo, although never defined as a dogma, continued strong in Catholic theology up until the present, that is until Vatican II. Today the emphasis has shifted from the static notion of baptism as one specific ceremony which eradicates sin to an initiation into a way of life. The spirit of the early Church has been reintroduced. Since it is a dramatic change in our understanding, Catholics today need to be informed and updated. Baptism is no automatic rite which is doled out on the spot, nor does it guarantee that one will live the Christian life.

Vatican II, in the revision of the Rite of Baptism, emphasizes the role of the parents to provide continuing faith formation for the child. As a result, parents today, in order to have their child baptized, must undergo preparation for the sacrament by instruction. If the parents' faith life is in question, the priest has a right to delay the baptism of the child until guaranteed that the child will be raised in the faith through the parents' example.

The Church, too, is aware of the danger of baptizing merely because that is the thing to do. Because of this new approach, baptism is given after the parents have been prepared. Parishes set up certain times for instruction, and a child may therefore be several months old before he or she is baptized.

Limbo   *A term used in the Middle Ages and later in an attempt to explain the eternal destiny of unbaptized children who died; a state of natural and eternal happiness*

Saint Augustine   *Saint from Hippo in North Africa, 354–430; a Doctor of the Church whose many writings have greatly influenced the theology of many Christian Churches*

Baptism is also admittance into the community of faith. The new ritual recommends baptism be celebrated at a solemn ceremony in the presence of the worshipping community. Many parishes baptize during the Sunday liturgy. This practice demonstrates the role the parish community plays in one's faith development.

Sponsors for baptism are required to act as role models and support in the faith. Ordinarily, two persons who are active in a Church can be sponsors. One must be Catholic; the other can belong to another Church.

Since a person's name is of significance, it has been the custom to name the child after a saint. The Code of Canon Law states that parents "take care that a name is not given which is foreign to Christian sentiment."[2]

Rite of Christian Initiation of Adults

An unbaptized adult who wishes to enter the Catholic Church goes through a process of faith discernment called the RCIA (Rite of Christian Initiation of Adults). The entire process is sometimes called the catechumenate. The RCIA is often adapted for use with baptized adults, but different rites are used.

The restoration of the catechumenate, the ancient mode of admitting converts, is one of the most significant changes following Vatican II. The process of formation involves various elements: pre-evangelization, instruction, formation, prayer, celebration, and the experience of community.

The RCIA is not just a means for admitting converts, but it is an opportunity for the entire faith community to be renewed and to grow and share the faith. The concept is still new, and parishes have just recently introduced it into their communities. The process centers on the faith journey to which each of us is called. The RCIA, when developed, can be a vital basis for continuing adult spiritual formation, for one can always grow more in one's faith.

---

2. The Canon Law Society of Great Britain and Ireland, *The Code of Canon Law* (London: Collins Liturgical Publications, 1983), p. 158, c.855.

Sponsor   *1. A godparent at baptism; 2. A person who accompanies another preparing for the Sacraments of Initiation, or for confirmation or marriage*

Confirmation

At Pentecost, the promise of Jesus to send the Spirit was fulfilled. The apostles witnessed to their faith and laid hands on fellow believers who also spread the faith. This laying on of hands and the gift of the Spirit given in conjunction with baptism gradually evolved into a separate ritual, probably when infant baptism became common.

Confirmation became the sacrament of the Holy Spirit, strengthening one in the faith. After the Council of Trent, which emphasized its sacramental character, confirmation was seen as a powerful antidote to false beliefs. It was the sacrament that enabled one to defend the faith and be willing to give one's life, if necessary.

A confirmed person, like a soldier, guarded his or her faith. The soldier image, a carryover from the Crusades, was reinforced when the bishop gave a slight slap on the cheek as part of the ritual. Most Catholics confirmed before Vatican II remember that aspect more than the deeper significance of the sacrament.

Confirmation is still undergoing development since Vatican II. Since one is strengthened in one's faith and since confirmation is the free, responsible acceptance of one's Christian commitment, one who receives confirmation ought to make a conscious choice.

Confirmation needs to be carried into practical action in one's life. Renewal in the theology of the Holy Spirit and the vitality of the charismatic movement has provided deeper spiritual dimensions toward approaching confirmation more meaningfully.

Eucharist

Although we dealt with the Eucharist as liturgy in the chapter on Catholic worship, we explore the Eucharist in this section as the sacrament received by the faithful in Communion.

The Body and Blood of Christ, under the appearances of bread and wine as Communion, are ordinarily received during the liturgy. It may be distributed outside of the Mass for a special reason, for example, to the sick or homebound.

In order to receive Communion, a Catholic must be in the state of grace, that is, in friendship with the Lord. Out of respect for the sacramental presence, one stays away from solid food and drink for one hour before receiving Communion. Water and medicine may be taken.

Communion is usually given in the form of bread on the tongue or in the hand. Often the faithful are offered the opportunity to receive the wine from the chalice. One does not receive "more" Communion; receiving in the two forms adds solemnity.

Communion is available every day, and Catholics are encouraged to receive at the Eucharistic Liturgy. One may receive twice a day on special occasions.

In former times, Catholics refrained from receiving Communion because they deemed themselves unworthy. Pope Pius X, in 1914, encouraged frequent and daily Communion. He also began the practice of admitting young children to Communion, which up to then was first received in the teen years. The celebration of young children receiving their First Holy Communion remains a solemn and inspiring ceremony in Catholic parishes.

Sacraments of a State of Life

The Sacraments of **Holy Orders** and **Matrimony** sanctify one's vocation in life. The sacraments bring Divine Life and these two sacraments make sacred the origins of life, human and spiritual.

Matrimony

The Catholic Church has always taken most seriously the bond of marriage, based on the scriptural admonition, "What God has united, human beings must not divide." (Matthew 19:6) Not only is marriage a lasting bond between two people, it is a loving, covenant relationship to be compared to Christ's relationship with the Church. In fact, marriage is so serious and sacred that legislation in Canon Law is detailed in more than one hundred canons (canons 1055–1165).

Holy Orders   *The sacrament by which a deacon, priest, or bishop is ordained*

Matrimony   *The marriage contract celebrated sacramentally*

When one obtains a civil **divorce,** the Church holds firm that the bonds of a valid marriage remain. In recent years, in an attempt to forestall broken marriages, the Church requires an intense preparation before marriage.

The Church has granted **annulments** for centuries, but more frequently since Vatican II. In an annulment, after scrutiny and examination of the parties involved, the Church declares that no sacramental marriage ever existed, due to some hidden defect or impediment present from the beginning.

A Catholic marriage usually takes place at a special **Nuptial Mass.** The couple are encouraged to plan and prepare the liturgy in order to make the event more meaningful.

Although the Church encourages Catholics to marry Catholics, the attitude toward marriages of couples with different faiths has changed. Formerly, a Catholic who married one of a different faith could not get married within the church sanctuary, but only in the rectory or sacristy of the church. In the ecumenical climate of Vatican II, mixed marriages may take place in church with nuptial solemnity. A Catholic may also get married in the church of the other party, or elsewhere, provided the form of the celebration of marriage conforms to Canon Law.

With the rising divorce rate and breakdown of family life, much pastoral work needs to be done concerning marriage. Ministry to the divorced, counseling on family planning and human sexuality, and adequate preparation programs are areas demanding special attention when working to promote the sacredness of marriage.

Holy Orders

This sacrament has been dealt with in detail in chapter IV.

Annulment   *The declaration that a marriage is null and void because it was never validly entered into, due to an invalidating impediment*

Divorce   *The dissolution of a marriage*

Nuptial Mass   *The Mass at which a marriage is celebrated*

Sacraments of Healing

Healing both of soul and body has always been part of the Christian concern. During his life, Jesus spent much time healing the sick and befriending the sinner. The Church today continues this healing mission of Christ through the Sacrament of the Anointing of the Sick and the Sacrament of Reconciliation.

Sacrament of Reconciliation

We have all experienced the soothing effect of the words, "I'm sorry" and "I forgive you." To heal and be healed releases a sense of vitality and freedom. How lighthearted one feels after making up after an argument.

The Church, throughout the years, has recognized that Jesus' healing power frees one from the guilt of sin. A variety of ways have been used to bring the forgiveness of sin to believers.

The early Christians committed their lives so wholeheartedly to Christ that, once baptized, they were expected to live sinless lives. Many did so to the extent of martyrdom. For the less perfect, forgiveness was received during the Eucharist, in fraternal correction, and in community gatherings.

During the third century, if guilty of a sin which brought public scandal, the sinner was excommunicated from the assembly. Only after a period of public **penance,** wearing sackcloth and ashes, and absolution by the bishop, was one readmitted to the community.

However, public repentance soon lost its symbolic meaning, and fewer sinners made use of it. Many postponed repentance, hoping to receive forgiveness on their deathbed. Most Christians had no need for public penitence, because the majority never committed the sins which required public penance. Since most Christians failed sometimes, they sought other ways of being forgiven. The Church set apart a penitential time for public sinners, forty days before Easter. By the fourth century, this period of penance, **Lent,** was observed by all Christians.

Lent   *The six plus weeks from Ash Wednesday to the celebration of the Lord's Supper on Holy Thursday; a liturgical season of preparation for Easter*

Penance   *Acts of reparation*

· During the sixth century, Irish monks introduced the custom of private confession as part of retreats and spiritual guidance. Soon the custom spread, and private confession became common.

By the twelfth century, the Church recognized the benefits of private confession, and it became the standard form of sacramental forgiveness. The Fourth Lateran Council prescribed that if one is guilty of serious sin, he or she must confess at least once a year.

As the practice continued, the priest soon acted as the judge who doled out fitting penances for atonement. Abuses began to creep in, such as the wealthy paying the poor to do their penances. By the time of the Council of Trent, confession became so standardized that priests were given lists of sins with corresponding penances. A person confessed; the priest consulted his book. Every sin had an appropriate penance prescribed by the book.

To preserve anonymity, confessionals, enclosed alcoves, became part of every Catholic church. Such a mode of confession led to the perception of the sacrament as an impersonal ritual with emphasis on the reciting of one's sins. Rote confessions gave little concern for the healing forgiveness of Christ. The renewal of Vatican II has attempted to restore the healing forgiveness as the purpose of the sacrament.

The sacrament, which was formerly called the Sacrament of Penance or Confession, is now the Sacrament of Reconciliation. A word introduced into Catholic vocabulary recently, *reconciliation* means "to go with again." It points to harmony and peace in all relationships. One needs to be reconciled with God, others, and within oneself.

Private confession is still the accepted mode for receiving sacramental forgiveness, but today the emphasis lies in the celebration of the forgiveness and healing power of Christ rather than on the recital of sins. Confession to a priest brings the healing of Christ to us through the power of holy orders. The priest is also the representative of the community who accepts the sinner back. Sin breaks down the intensity of goodness in the community of believers. When one is forgiven by God through the priest, who represents the community, goodness is restored and the Body of Christ is built up. No sin is entirely private or personal. Every small, less-than-perfect act contributes to sinfulness in the world. Any sinful attitude diminishes the strength of good and intensifies evil.

Only recently have we begun to look seriously at this communal aspect of sin. When we speak of sin, we ought not merely think of specific actions, but also of a subtle attitude of sinfulness. In a practical way, when one confesses, one need not recite a list of specific sins, but instead ask oneself: "What habit or tendency within me needs conversion? How can I be a more loving person? Where have I contributed to the evils in the world? What area of my life calls me to conversion and change? Why do I react in a less-than-perfect way? Where do I need healing?"

Responding to these questions is one way to be attuned to sinfulness, rather than sin in a private sense only. Confession can become more profitable spiritually when, in an informal way, one relates to the priest and begs for Christ's healing forgiveness.

The priest may give helpful advice and encouragement and absolve in Jesus' name. The penance may be given by the priest or he may ask the penitent to choose it. Either way, the penance shows concretely that one plans to turn from sinful ways.

This approach to sacramental forgiveness requires more soul-searching and effort. And if confessions are not as frequent, hopefully they are deeper and more meaningful.

This revised Rite of Reconciliation may be conducted in several ways. The traditional anonymous confession may be preferred by those who are used to it and feel comfortable with it. The face-to-face confession, in which the priest and penitent sit informally, provides an atmosphere conducive to a true healing experience. Some Catholics may hesitate to try it, but once one experiences confession in this manner, as a spiritual healing, one probably will continue choosing that method.

Since there is a renewed awareness of the communal aspect of sin, communal penance services, at which the community joins in prayer before and after private confession, have proven beneficial toward making confession more meaningful. **General absolution,** given *en masse* without private confession, is reserved for exceptional situations.

But penance is not just a ritual. It is part of the rhythm of our lives. We are continuously called to conversion. We will never reach the point when we can sit back and say, "I've made it." The call of Christ to radical discipleship demands that we can always be better. Sacramental forgiveness and healing prods us on.

General Absolution *The form of sacramental forgiveness of sins given when individual confession by a large number of people is not possible*

Sacrament of the Anointing of the Sick

Since physical health is necessary for wholeness and well-being, the Church offers solace in sickness through the Sacrament of the Anointing of the Sick. **Anointing with oil** is an ancient custom and symbolizes strength as well as power to cure. Since apostolic times, anointing of the sick has been used by the faithful. In the Epistle of James we read: "Is there anyone who is sick? He should send for the church elders. . . ." (James 5:14) Gradually the ritual evolved into a sacramental rite which was used by priests. By the Middle Ages, extreme unction was listed among the seven sacraments.

When this sacrament was administered only to the dying, it was called **extreme unction** or the **last rites.** Today, with sacramental renewal, it is called the anointing of the sick and includes all who need healing, especially the sick, the elderly, the chronically ill, and anyone for whom healing may be appropriate. The priest prays over the one to be anointed and then anoints the forehead and palms with oil which was specially blessed by the bishop on Holy Thursday.

The sacrament, as the continuing healing presence of Christ, may at times effect a physical cure or improvement, but more often it provides spiritual strength to bear sickness. The sacrament reminds us of the saving value of suffering, in union with the sufferings of Jesus.

The sacrament can be given to an individual or a group. A communal anointing service makes visible the support of the community and brings out the ecclesial dimension of the sacraments. In the communal anointing, the whole Church prays for wholeness.

Many parishes periodically celebrate the communal anointing of the sick in the context of the liturgy. This provides support to the elderly and sick and, at the same time, it reminds all the people of God of our human condition of limitation and mortality.

Anointing with Oil *An external sign used in several sacraments: baptism, confirmation, holy orders, and anointing of the sick*

Extreme Unction *A previously used term for the Sacrament of Anointing of the Sick*

Last Rites *Sacraments of Reconciliation, Eucharist, and Anointing given to a dying person; the term itself is no longer officially used by the Church*

Even though the sacrament may restore a person to health, the sacramental grace enables one to reflect on the reality of death. A separate ritual provides appropriate prayers if one receives the sacrament in danger of death. Eucharist received at this time is called **Viaticum.**

In connection with the Sacrament of the Anointing of the Sick, it is helpful to note that there is a renewed interest in healing of body and soul through the power of the Holy Spirit. The charismatic movement has emphasized the gift of healing in its spirituality and sense of lived faith. Nonsacramental healing services are often conducted as part of charismatic gatherings. This new heightened awareness of the power of the Holy Spirit, along with a renewed theology of the Sacrament of the Anointing of the Sick, deepens our insights and faith in the healing power of God within our midst.

Catholic Attitude toward Death

The Catholic attitude toward death takes on deeper significance through the death and resurrection of Jesus. A Catholic believes that at death, "Life is changed, not ended." (Preface from the Catholic Burial Rite) Death is a passage to a new and fuller life, and ultimately to resurrection and eternal union with God.

"If the spirit of God, who raised Jesus from death, lives in you, then he who raised Christ from death will also give life to your mortal bodies by the presence of his Spirit in you."—Romans 8:11

Although death brings a deep sense of loss, faith provides solace and strength. The Church emphasizes "life" in the funeral liturgy. The resurrection is the theme, and the readings, hymns, and prayers reflect the overall tone of expectant joy. At Mass, the priest wears white vestments symbolizing joy. The Paschal Candle is lit, and Easter hymns are often sung.

Catholics believe the dead can be helped and assisted by our prayerful remembrance. And so the custom of giving stipends for Masses at which the dead person will be remembered at the liturgy is common and appropriate.

Viaticum *The Sacrament of the Eucharist received by a dying person*

Catholics are buried with honor and respect in a grave site which is blessed. In times past, it was customary to have the cemetery next to the church. Today, cemeteries are more commonly shared by a group of churches or the diocese. Mausoleums, separate structures in which the dead are interred above ground, are also becoming more common. **Cremation,** formerly forbidden, is now allowed.

Conclusion

The sacraments remain for Catholics the definite assurance that Jesus is with us in a special manner, in special times, and for special needs. The sacraments are encounters with the Risen Christ present through the signs and symbols. We are accepted into the faith community, strengthened, nurtured, forgiven, healed, committed in love, and directed through the sacramental rituals. From birth to death Jesus remains with the believers in living signs of his constant presence. With the sacraments, our friendship with Jesus remains vibrant. Sacraments fulfill special needs and will always be Christ's special moments of meeting us in love.

Cremation   *The burning of human remains, once strictly forbidden by the Church when it was seen as a denial of immortality*

VII

What Role Does the Bible Play in a Catholic's Faith Life?

Bible—Tradition—Hebrew Scriptures— Christian Scriptures—Old Testament— New Testament—Israelites— Alexandrian Canon—Epistles— Septuagint—Gospels—Apocrypha— Vulgate—Fundamentalists

Introduction

Catholics have always revered the **Bible** as the inspired Word of God. Along with Tradition, the Scriptures are the chief sources of God's revelation. The Bible has a prominent place in Catholic homes, an honored volume wherein dates of family events are often recorded. It is respected as God's Word. However, often it is treated with the respect one may have for royalty: You admire, but you would never invite them into your home for tea; you feel uneasy.

That is how the Bible has been treated by many Catholics. One needs to treat the Bible with the familiarity and friendliness you extend to a friend sitting at your kitchen table chatting about ordinary daily life. The Bible ought to be part of one's personal spirituality in this familiar way.

In this chapter, we present the Bible as a friend one can meet. We explore its essence—God speaking to us in our situation today. We consider how the Bible has changed and evolved through the years. In order to understand it better, we clarify some points. We conclude with practical hints on how to make the Bible part of our spiritual lives and how to blend it into our lives as good neighbors with respect to its royal origins.

Nature of the Bible

The Bible, in the form we know it today, is a book divided into two parts. The first part, the **Hebrew Scriptures,** or the **Old Testament** as many Christians call it, is the written record of the Jewish people from **Abraham** (1800 B.C.E.) until the **Maccabean Era** (168 B.C.E.). The second part of the Christian Bible is the **New Testament,** or **Christian Scriptures,** which contains the life and works of Jesus as well as the faith experience of the early Christians until about A.D. 100.

Abraham *The father of the Jewish people, traditionally understood to be the earliest ancestor, with his wife Sarah, of the Hebrews or Israelites*

Bible *The Sacred Scriptures, Old and New Testaments; the Word of God*

Christian Scriptures *The books of the New Testament in the Bible*

Hebrew Scriptures *The Old Testament of the Bible*

Maccabean Era *A period of time in the second century B.C.E. when the last Old Testament books were first written*

New Testament *The Christian Scriptures of the Bible*

Old Testament *The books of Hebrew Scriptures found in the Bible*

The Bible is inspired because, through the words of human authors, God has revealed His will and plan for the destiny of people. The Bible, written under the guidance of the Holy Spirit, remains a vital source of God's revelation to humans.

We say the Bible is the Word of God. Through the basic form of human communication of words, we humans actually give part of our inner selves to another. Words convey something within us. God, in sharing His love for people, has used the normal human frame of reference to reveal Himself.

An appropriate way to consider the nature of the Bible is to see it as a story. Through stories, we come to grips with reality, keep experiences alive, and preserve precious moments. Elie Wiesel, the famous Jewish storyteller, notes, "God made man because God loves stories." We can add: We have the Bible because God and people love stories.

The Bible, like all good stories, has a basic plot. When left to our own imagining, we grope and stumble trying to discover the Divine. Reason and logic cannot fathom how deep is the Creator's love. God knew, too, that people could not fall in love with a formula or abstract concept. At a certain time in history, God stepped into the human sphere in hopes of establishing a loving covenant with people.

In Jewish tradition, the man who noticed was Abraham. God's way was not so direct that Abraham had no need of faith, but His way of revealing His love was enough to guide Abraham in his search for God. Abraham believed and responded, and his faith was rewarded. He became the father of a great nation. God continued to extend Himself in history in the lives of the Jewish people, the **Israelites.**

The basic plot of the Bible revolves around God's love for people and the extent to which He showed His love despite the refusals and backslidings of people.

The Bible, like any story, has a beginning and an end. It begins with the powerful voice of God reaching out in love to create, "Let there be light." (Genesis 1:3) It ends with a pleaful human sigh, "Come, Lord Jesus!" (Revelation 22:20) The Bible opens with the Lord and a solitary human being in a garden; it closes with a multitude praising God in the heavenly city. It begins with God reaching out to people and ends with people approaching God. Between the pages, there is a constant interplay of God and humans, with a whole cast of characters emerging.

Israelites *The Jewish people; commonly used term in the Old Testament*

The people who grace the pages of the Bible are all that the human person is anytime and anywhere he or she accepts or rejects God. We need not be shocked at the human elements we find in the Bible. Sinners and saints alike portray the whole gamut of the human condition. There is faith and despair, war and peace, hate and love. The people try to heed what God is saying, but sometimes the will of God is misread.

Fearful, boneheaded, stubborn, and rebellious—the people find the loving God too much. There are the weak who find the Word of God too challenging. Some faithful few always remain steadfast.

Prophets, such as **Jeremiah,** translate the experience of God into a language the people can grasp. Poets sing songs. Sages give life a deeper meaning.

The characters who appear in the Bible walk not with the elegant finesse of stained-glass figures. They are flesh-and-blood persons whose faith in God and humans is put to the test.

God reveals Himself in many ways. He comes in dreams, oracles, prophecies, and most often amid one's daily chores. There are monologues, dialogues, soliloquies, sermons, and silence. We meet God and humans in the desert, in cities, on mountains, by the roadside. In fact, the God of the Bible bursts in wherever people are. Behind the diverse personalities, events, and attitudes, God reaches out from every page of the Bible to speak of His ways with people.

Every story demands movement toward a climax. As the Bible story unfolds, God reaches out in love with ever greater intensity. He sends His Son, Jesus, who proclaims the Good News and reveals most fully who God is. In living among people as a human, Jesus proves that the divine and the human can be joined. Teilhard de Chardin points out that when Christ came, a new dimension of reality entered the world. The cosmos is "Christ-ified," raised to the level of the divine.

But the Bible is unlike other stories in one aspect. It cannot be read as a past historical document, something which happened to those people of another age and another culture. It cannot be read in the third person as they, them, he, she. The Bible is no dead letter. It is God acting today. The characters are the models and prototypes God used to show people of all time His love and how He works with humans.

Jeremiah   *Old Testament prophet of Judah who preached the love of God; a major prophet*

We need to get caught up in the drama of the Bible and identify with the people, the miracles, and the saving events. We all have our passovers, exoduses, transfigurations, and resurrections in the course of our ordinary lives. The Bible allows no spectators. Everyone is part of salvation history. When we read the Bible, we must consider it as the present tense, for God is working now.

Origins of the Scriptures

The Bible did not begin as a full-blown book, but as an experience of God lived by the Israelites and early Christians. These people came to understand God's presence in their midst in the events, persons, daily happenings, and miracles. They interpreted these saving acts of God and passed on their faith by word of mouth. These ancient peoples were not the paper-and-pen generation as are we; they relied on their sharp memories.

Gradually, at significant times, the Israelites committed to writing certain parts of their heritage; for example, the Ten Commandments and parts of the Torah were written first. When the nation formed and kings ruled, court histories and chronicles were kept. During the Exile, their heritage was preserved by completing the history and writing down the words of the prophets. The writing was done in Hebrew on scrolls and taken back to Palestine after the Exile (537 B.C.E.).

Other Jews who had fled to Egypt translated the Hebrew Scriptures into Greek in a version called the **Septuagint** or the **Alexandrian Canon.** This copy included seven books which were not in the Hebrew or Palestinian Canon. (This is a significant detail in later biblical development.)

The New Testament, too, developed gradually. The early Christian communities, when they gathered for the Lord's Supper, circulated the letters Paul sent to the various communities of faith. The groups found Paul's letters, written between A.D. 52–64 to be valuable and practical for their living out of Christ's teachings. These **epistles** are the earliest works of the New Testament.

Alexandrian Canon   *The collection of Hebrew Scriptures translated into Greek; Septuagint*

Epistles   *Early letters of the Christian Church included in the Christian Scriptures*

Septuagint   *The Hebrew Scriptures translated into Greek; also called the Alexandrian Canon*

As the Christian communities spread to other parts of the Empire, the apostles and disciples took with them their memories and the collections of sayings, episodes, miracles, and faith experiences of Jesus. These were proclaimed to the faithful. But time wore on and the first witnesses were dying. Collections of the Good News, **"Gospels,"** were written and circulated among the Christian communities. Finally, four Gospels were accepted by the community as most authentic because they were intimately connected with the apostles, and developed in four major areas: **Matthew** (Jerusalem), Mark (Rome), **Luke** (Antioch), and **John** (Ephesus). Later, about A.D. 100, the **Book of Revelation** or the **Apocalypse** was added because people believed that the second coming of Christ was imminent. The Book of Revelation, always open to many interpretations, ultimately portrays the constant struggle between good and evil.

The twenty-seven books of the New Testament—four Gospels, Acts of the Apostles, epistles of Paul and other early Christian leaders, and the Apocalypse—are recognized and accepted by all Christians.

Apocalypse   *Book of Revelation in the New Testament*

Book of Revelation   *Apocalypse; highly symbolic and secretive book which closes the New Testament*

Gospel of John   *A proclamation of the Good News of Jesus to the people of Ephesus, included in the New Testament*

Gospel of Luke   *A proclamation of the Good News of Jesus to the people of Antioch, included in the New Testament*

Gospel of Mark   *A proclamation of the Good News of Jesus to the people of Rome, included in the New Testament*

Gospel of Matthew   *A proclamation of the Good News of Jesus to the people of Jerusalem, included in the New Testament*

Gospels   *Proclamations of the Good News of Jesus; four are included in the New Testament*

Development of the Scriptures

These early Scriptures were written on scrolls. To be preserved, they were painstakingly copied. Later, this work was taken up by the monks. Although there are manuscripts which date back to the early days, we have no originals of the Scriptures.

When Latin became the common language, **Pope Damasus** commissioned **Saint Jerome,** around A.D. 383, to translate the Bible into Latin. This version became the official Christian Bible known as the **Vulgate.**

When Saint Jerome translated, he used the Greek text of the Scriptures. The Old Testament Canon in Greek contained the books of **Wisdom, Sirach (Ecclesiasticus), Baruch, Judith, Tobias,** and the two books of **Maccabees,** which were not in the Hebrew Scriptures. Consequently, translations of later times, which reverted to

Baruch   *Old Testament book not part of the Protestant versions, one of the Apocrypha*

Ecclesiasticus   *Old Testament book also called Sirach*

Judith   *Old Testament book not part of the Protestant versions, one of the Apocrypha*

Maccabees   *Two Old Testament books not part of the Protestant versions, two of the Apocrypha*

Pope Damasus   *Pope at the time of the Ecumenical Council Constantinople in 381; a saint*

Saint Jerome   *The saint who translated the books of the Bible into Latin in the fourth century; called the Vulgate*

Sirach   *Ecclesiasticus, Old Testament book not part of the Protestant versions, one of the Apocrypha*

Tobias   *Old Testament book not part of the Protestant versions, one of the Apocrypha*

Vulgate   *The Latin translation of the Bible made by Saint Jerome*

Wisdom   *Old Testament book not part of the Protestant versions, one of the Apocrypha*

the Hebrew Canon, were minus the seven books in the Greek Old Testament. These seven books came to be known as the **Apocrypha.**

Because **Martin Luther** used the Hebrew version in translating the Bible into German during the Reformation, the Protestant Bible had seven less books than the Catholic Vulgate which was based on the Greek. Today however, many Protestant Bibles include the Apocrypha.

In the Middle Ages, the Bible was not widely read because most people were illiterate. It was passed on by storytellers. Some peasants knew the 150 **psalms** from memory and recited them as they tilled the fields. Art and stained-glass windows depicted Bible scenes and miracle plays acted out the Bible in drama presentations. The **Passion Play at Oberammergau** began in 1633 and continues to this day.

The Reformation stressed the Word of God as the sole authority. The Bible was translated into the language of the people, and theology was based on scriptural teachings.

The Catholic reaction to the Reformation in the Council of Trent upheld Scripture and Tradition as equal sources of God's revelation. The emphasis of faith focused on the sacraments, doctrines, and laws. The Bible thus became secondary. Contrary to popular belief, the Bible was not forbidden to Catholics, but the faithful were cautioned to read and use only approved versions. This caveat contributed greatly to the Bible being relegated to a lesser position in the Catholic Church. With the coming of history as an exact science, the Bible was passed on as "Bible history."

In the early part of the twentieth century, renewed interest in the Bible grew due to archaeology and form criticism. Scholars discovered how the Bible was compiled and the culture in which it developed. Many efforts at collaboration remained in the realm of scholarly research until Vatican II.

Apocrypha   *Seven books of the Old Testament that were in the Septuagint and are in the Catholic versions of the Bible, but not officially in Protestant versions*

Martin Luther   *(d. 1546) Augustinian monk who was eventually responsible for starting the Protestant Reformation; founder of the Lutheran Church*

Passion Play at Oberammergau   *A type of miracle play begun in 1633 and continuing to the present*

Psalms   *The book of 150 hymn prayers in the Old Testament*

Vatican II attempted to restore the Bible to its rightful place. Newer translations were commissioned. Catholics now are exposed to the Bible as never before. The first part of the liturgy is called the Liturgy of the Word. Bible study groups have been formed to make the Bible more understandable for Catholics.

Catholics have been encouraged to take up the Bible and use it in their personal prayer life. Research continues, and today Bibles are prepared with the collaboration of Jewish, Catholic, and Protestant scholars. The Bible is the avenue through which **ecumenical** dialogue reaches toward a common theological understanding.

The Scriptures in Personal Spirituality

In the "Dogmatic Constitution on Divine Revelation," the Sacred Synod proposes: "all the Christian faithful . . . to learn by frequent reading of the divine Scriptures. . . .'Ignorance of the Scriptures is ignorance of Christ.' "[1]

Vatican II encourages a deeper understanding of the Bible through liturgy and also by devotional reading. The Bible is unlike other spiritual reading books which we can dismiss. The Bible is God's Word which we cannot ignore. Since Catholics have not been accustomed to take up the Scriptures on their own for private devotion and prayers, we now present some practical hints on how to profit from Scripture reading.

First, choose a Bible with which you feel comfortable. There are many versions today that serve various needs. The Bible is also available in different formats. There are the large volumes which include numerous explanatory notes and cross references. Smaller pocket-sized versions are convenient to carry with you. The *New American Bible* is used in the liturgy.

---

1. Walter M. Abbott, S.J., ed. "Dogmatic Constitution on Divine Revelation," *The Documents of Vatican II* (New York: America Press, 1966), p. 127, article 25.

Ecumenical *Promoting unity among Christians*

No matter what Bible you select, make the Bible your friend. Feel free to underline and make notations for your prayer. "A Bible that's falling apart is owned by a person who isn't (falling apart)." The Bible is sacred, but need not be a museum piece. The Bible ought to be used.

As you now have your Bible, where should you begin? The Bible is not meant to be read from cover to cover. Its purpose is to help us relate to God better and to see God's works with humans. Begin with prayer, asking God to guide you to hear Him speak to you now, in your situation.

Choose a selection to read. It could be either a liturgical selection in the Mass, or another section on which you decide. Read the selection slowly. Put yourself into the picture. Can you relate to anyone or to the situation? What is the message being related? Why is this story part of Scripture? What does it tell about the relation between people and God or about people's sinful or saintly attitude?

Pause and reflect. The Scriptures are God speaking and we need to take time to listen. Maybe an insight which you have never thought of before will help you in your life.

If you are not familiar with the portion of Scripture you have chosen, read the introduction to learn why the author wrote the book, what message he wished to convey, and the literary form which he used in writing it. The Bible, like other literary works, is written in a unique style. The section you are reading may be a parable, a historically accurate account, or a myth which brings out a deeper truth through the avenue of a story.

Consider all that God or Jesus says as directed to you. Ask yourself what it means for your spiritual benefit. Savor it; do not devour it. Make it a habit as part of personal prayer to spend some time each day with the Bible. You will soon find it to be a valuable friend and support.

Another way to become more familiar with the Scriptures lies in developing your sense of hearing. The Scriptures are read at Mass and are to be listened to and heard. If you hone your hearing and concentrate on what is being read, you may well come away from the liturgy with a new insight. You listen, and one day you actually may *hear* something the Lord speaks just to you.

Catholics need to realize that the Bible cannot be taken literally. The message is more important than the words through which the message is conveyed. When confronted by **fundamentalists** who believe every word is meant as stated, one need not argue, but simply say, "To me, God seems to be saying. . . ." This attitude forestalls unnecessary theological squabbles.

The Bible, we believe, is God's revelation. But not all the truths Catholics believe are directly stated in the Bible. Therefore, one cannot use the Bible as a proof-text.

In order to understand the Bible more fully, it would be profitable to take a course that gives an overview of the Bible, how it was assembled, the culture, and the geography. This is a valuable topic for adult education enrichment courses.

It is also beneficial to join a Bible study group. However, it is necessary for the leader of such a group to have an educated understanding of Scripture. Otherwise, the group may encounter interpretation difficulties.

Because of increased cooperation between Jewish, Protestant, and Catholic scholars, the Bible is becoming more integrated. Many Bibles include all books, including the Apocrypha.

Conclusion

The Bible, then, is much more than a static depository of revelation. It is a meaningful instrument to strengthen our relationship with God and to learn how God works in our lives today. In the Bible, we discover all the demands that a loving relationship entails: response, discovery, growth, disappointments, change, and new insights. In our pilgrimage of faith, we all have our passovers, exoduses, and calls to conversion. From an alien land of sin we are called to the Promised Land of the covenant.

It is when we allow the Lord to break into our lives that we appreciate the full import of the Scriptures. God speaks to us; He heals, challenges, invites, and instructs us in His ways through the Bible. God reaches out again and again in love to the world through His Sacred Word. We need to respond. We need to dust off our Bibles and pick up the story of God's love.

Fundamentalists *Generally refers to those who adhere to a literal interpretation of the Bible*

VIII

Why Do Catholics Use Sacramentals and Honor Saints?

**Indulgence—Benediction—Forty Hours'
Devotion—Novenas—Blessings—Sign of
the Cross—Holy Water—Chrism—Ash
Wednesday—Palm Sunday—Cross—
Crucifix—Chi-Rho—Council of Nicaea—
Iconoclasm—Scapular—Advent—Holy
Days—Church Calendar—Mary—
Rosary—Virgin Birth—Apparition—
Communion of Saints—Canonization**

Introduction

We know the feeling a favorite photo evokes. It
connects us with a person or place that is important to us.
Souvenirs, albums, autographs, and memorabilia link us
with something that is special in our lives, provides
meaningfulness, and preserves a precious memory.

We also use words, gestures, symbols, and objects to keep the presence and thought of God alive and to serve as constant reminders of His love. In addition to the seven sacraments, which are the Church's special signs of God's actions, Catholics use **sacramentals** to keep in touch with spiritual things.

We will examine the nature of sacramentals and the role they serve in a Catholic's faith life. In this chapter, we also explain some of the common sacramentals as well as other things and people considered sacred. The saints and Mary hold a special place in the faith, as persons who remind us of God.

Nature of Sacramentals

Sacramentals "make sacred" the ordinary things of the world and bring a sacred dimension into our daily actions. These realities are called sacramental because, like the sacraments, they effect a spiritual result.

But sacramentals differ from sacraments in several ways. Sacramentals are not sacred in themselves, but they signify spiritual effects through the faith of the believer and through the prayer of the Church. Sacraments are sacred actions, independent of personal motives. For example, if an unworthy person who receives Communion receives the Body and Blood of Christ, his or her unworthiness does not affect the sacrament's reality.

There are seven sacraments, but sacramentals cannot be counted. Many have been used a long time as traditions, while others may last a short while or be used in only a specific area.

Sacraments are essential to Catholic belief and practice, while sacramentals are pious traditions. Even though approved by the Church, they are not essential doctrines. What sacramentals signify is based on belief and the prayer of the Church, but their use or acceptance as a practice is optional.

Sacramental   *An object, action, or blessing which is a sacred sign of spiritual favors from God*

Sacramentals assume many forms: devotional exercises, blessings, prayers, actions, objects, places, times. Common universal sacramentals often carry **indulgences.** This means that the Church affirms that their devout use will help one in a spiritual way, or, to put it into theological language, they remit temporal punishment due for sin.

Catholics make use of sacramentals for spiritual solace, guidance, or help. In times of sickness, for instance, one who grasps a crucifix or prays the rosary may more easily accept the pain in a spirit of faith. Even though sacramentals are accessories to the faith, they serve as powerful aids toward a meaningful spiritual life.

Popular Devotional Exercises or Private Devotions

Catholic piety brings people together to pray for specific intentions. These devotions may honor or recall a particular saint, a specific aspect of the life of Christ or Mary, or a certain mystery or doctrine of faith. While many devotions have been replaced by liturgical celebrations since Vatican II, they still are valid prayer forms. Though they have decreased in number, many are still proper personal devotions.

Benediction

This devotion, which honors the Eucharistic Presence in a solemn way, began when the emphasis in piety focused on adoration. The large host is displayed in an ornate golden vessel called a **monstrance.** The faithful offer veneration through prayers, hymns,

Benediction   *A Eucharistic devotion which includes the exposition of the Blessed Sacrament in a monstrance*

Indulgence   *The remission of temporal punishment due for sins*

Monstrance   *An ornate golden vessel used for the exposition of the Blessed Sacrament*

and special recognition of God's greatness in the **Divine Praises.** A priest usually officiates and wears a large cape called a **cope.**

Forty Hours' Devotion

This devotion provides an opportunity for a more intense veneration of the Eucharist. For three days, the host is displayed in the monstrance and the faithful spend time in prayer. The finale usually consists of a solemn procession. Many parishes conduct this devotion once a year or on a modified scale.

Cope   *A cape-type vestment used for some religious ceremonies other than Mass*

Divine Praises   *A litany of praises said after Benediction of the Blessed Sacrament*

Forty Hours' Devotion   *A solemn exposition of the Blessed Sacrament for a period of forty hours*

Novenas

In imitation of the apostles who prayed for nine days before Pentecost, some Catholics pray **novenas** to specific saints for special intentions. Public novenas are held in church. Many Catholics also make private novenas, and many ethnic groups have favorite novenas.

Processions

In many religions, processions and pageantry add solemnity to a special feast or observance. Catholic Churches hold processions in church or outdoors, especially during the Forty Hours' Devotion and May processions in honor of Mary, or other processions in honor of a patron saint.

Other Devotions

Devotions which many Catholics make part of their spiritual life include: the rosary, stations of the cross, or congregational praying of the Divine Office or a simplified *Book of Christian Prayer*. Because the Bible has begun to play a greater role in Catholic spirituality, Bible vigils or Bible services are being used. Scripture passages, psalms, prayers, and reflections focus on a scriptural theme. Communal penance, services of healing, communal anointing of the sick, and charismatic prayer gained popularity following Vatican II.

Vatican II upholds that "Popular devotions of the Christian people are to be highly commended." Such devotions are encouraged, but must remain in proper perspective. "These devotions should be so drawn up that they harmonize with the liturgical seasons, are in accord with the sacred liturgy, are in some fashion derived from it, and lead the people to it, since the liturgy by its very nature far surpasses any of them."[1]

---

1. Walter M. Abbott, S. J., ed. "Constitution on the Sacred Liturgy," *The Documents of Vatican II* (New York: America Press, 1966), p. 143, article 13.

Novena   *Devotional prayers repeated for nine days or one day a week for nine weeks*

Gestures, Postures, and Blessings

Blessings are not unique to Catholic practices. Other religions also invoke the Divine for spiritual favors or honor. Catholics receive blessings through the ordained ministers of the Church: priests and deacons. Those ordained receive spiritual powers through holy orders, and so, when they bless, they bless in the name of Christ.

When a priest blesses during the celebration of the sacraments or at Mass, it is called a liturgical blessing. It is a private blessing when a person, place, or thing is blessed. Objects which are blessed and used for religious purposes are called sacramentals.

Blessings show humanity's dependence on God, but they also demonstrate God's concern about people's activities. And so, blessings can be given to pets, cars, homes, travelers, athletes, any thing or event which is important to people.

A blessing can be given by sprinkling with holy water, reciting a prayer, and by placing the hand on what is to be blessed and making the sign of the cross.

Other postures and gestures evoke spiritual feelings. A Catholic kneels for prayer and genuflects (touches one knee to the floor) before the tabernacle to show reverence. It is customary to bow the head at the name of Jesus.

Folding hands for prayer, with fingers intertwined, is a carryover from days when slaves were shackled as a sign of submission. Hands folded with fingers pointed upward symbolize that, in prayer, one's mind is raised to God. This symbol lies behind the shape of church steeples. A person can pray in any posture suitable and conducive to devotion.

Sign of the Cross

One of the most familiar and ancient Catholic gestures, the sign of the cross, in a concise way, expresses the basic truths of faith: the Trinity, and the redemption by Jesus on the cross, by the words, "In the name of the Father, and of the Son, and of the Holy Spirit. Amen."

Blessing   *A prayer, usually by a cleric, to invoke God's favor on persons or things*

Dipping the fingers into the holy water font on entering the church is a reminder of one's commitment to Christ in baptism. When it is done consciously with attention, this gesture serves as a powerful personal reminder of one's Christian faith. The sign of the cross is used in liturgical celebrations, sacraments, blessings, personal prayer, and devotions.

The most common way to make the sign of the cross is by touching the forehead, the chest, and the left and right shoulders with the fingertips of the open right hand. A priest blesses by tracing the cross in the air with his palm outstretched or while holding a crucifix. He may trace a cross with his thumb on the object he blesses.

Sacred Elements— Water, Oil, Light, Fire

Holy water is the universal symbol of spiritual cleansing. The custom of using holy water in the Church dates back to its early days. It is used in liturgical and devotional ways. Catholics bless themselves on entering a church and often keep holy water in their homes. It is kept in a font at a doorway, sprinkled before one retires, and used in times of illness or storms for God's protection. Of special significance is the water blessed during the Easter Vigil.

Oil has always symbolized strength. Holy oils used in rituals intend to portray spiritual strength. The oil of catechumens is used in baptism; the oil of the sick is used in anointing the ill and infirm. **Chrism,** a special mixture of olive oil and balm, is used in the other sacraments which require anointings: baptism, confirmation, and holy orders. Sacred oils are solemnly blessed by the bishop in the liturgy of Holy Thursday in the cathedral.

Light also plays an important role in religions. **Candles** are used not for purposes of illumination, although they may have originated for that reason. Candles symbolize joy and praise of God. They are used in the Catholic Church at all liturgical celebrations, as well as by persons for private devotion. Candles are blessed solemnly on

Candles, Blessed   *Sacramentals used in the liturgy of the Church*

Chrism   *Oil blessed by the bishop and used in the administering of several sacraments*

February 2, known as **Candlemas Day,** and the Paschal Candle is blessed at the Easter Vigil. Catholics keep blessed candles in their homes as protection and to be burned in times of need.

On **Ash Wednesday,** the beginning of Lent, Catholics receive blessed **ashes** made from the palms of the previous year. Signed on the forehead in the form of a cross, Catholics are reminded of their own death, "Remember, man, you are dust and to dust you will return." (Genesis 3:19) Another formula calls one to a change of heart and personal conversion, "Turn away from sin and be faithful to the gospel." (Mark 1:15) This practice helps Catholics begin Lent in a devotional way.

In many Christian Churches, palms are distributed on **Palm Sunday,** the week before Easter, in imitation of the crowds who carried palms when Jesus entered Jerusalem the week he died. Palms are taken home and kept, often near a crucifix. They are a sign of God's special protection.

Sacred Objects

The Cross or Crucifix

The most meaningful and sacred Christian symbol is the **cross.** In Roman times, it was an instrument of torture. After Christ was crucified, the cross was a forbidden symbol for the early Christians. They utilized other symbols: the fish, the dove, the lamb, and the **Chi-Rho** ☧ (the name of Christ).

Ashes *A sacramental made from palms of the previous year and used to mark the forehead in the sign of the cross on Ash Wednesday*

Ash Wednesday *The first day of Lent, a day of fast and abstinence*

Candlemas Day *February 2, the day on which candles are blessed*

Chi-Rho ☧ *or* ☦ *; Greek symbol for Christ*

Cross *Generally refers to the cross without the image of Jesus*

Palm Sunday *The last Sunday of Lent; recalls Jesus entry into Jerusalem*

After the fall of the Roman Empire, crosses depicted the Risen Lord in glory. Gradually, other forms evolved. In all, there are almost four hundred varieties of crosses, according to the *Heraldic Encyclopedia.*

Devotion to the Passion of Christ increased in the Middle Ages especially through the devotion to the sufferings of Christ popularized by Francis of Assisi. Crosses portrayed the Passion by affixing an image of the body of Jesus on the cross. This form is a **crucifix.**

After the Reformation, Protestants used the plain cross, and Catholics continued to use the crucifix. Many crosses today, in keeping with a different theological perspective, portray the Christ of the resurrection. Catholics use the crucifix at Mass, in processions, and in blessings. Most Catholics display a crucifix in their homes, and some wear one as a pendant. The cross continues to be a most sacred symbol, and it is considered most disrespectful to abuse it.

Statues, Medals, and Pictures

For many years, Catholics have also been using statues, medals, and pictures as objects of personal devotion. There was a time in the early Church when all representations were considered idolatrous. A heresy, called **iconoclasm,** condemned any use of statues or other representations of saints and angels, as well as of Christ. The **Council of Nicaea,** in 787, rejected iconoclasm as a false teaching. However, the Eastern Christians have refrained from using three-dimensional statues. To this day, two-dimensional icons are used by Eastern Orthodox and Eastern Catholics.

Scapulars, derived from the garb of monks, were used in early days so the laity could benefit from monastic prayers. The piece of small cloth, attached to strings and worn over the shoulders, was

Council of Nicaea *Council held in 787 which rejected iconoclasm and the heresy of adoptionism*

Crucifix *The cross with the image of Jesus crucified on it*

Iconoclasm *The heresy which condemned any use of statues or other representations of Christ, Mary, the angels, and saints*

Scapular *1. A shoulder-wide, long, outer garment which is part of many religious habits; 2. A sacramental, small imitation of the religious habit worn around the neck, usually by specific groups*

sacred because of the indulgences or spiritual favors they conveyed. There are many kinds of scapulars, the brown scapular and the green scapular being the most well-known. There are also scapular medals.

Religious Art

Although the Catholic Church has no specific art style of its own, many forms have been adopted from every age and culture. To be considered "religious," art should express faith, transcend the human, and render praise to God as a creative use of humanity's handiwork. Art, as a whole, is not limited to the spiritual realm, but religious art uses all of creation and many styles to portray humanity's inner spirit.

The Church accepts modern interpretations of its truths and keeps the current culture alive through its art. This is why the Church's vast storehouse of art treasures is valuable. It is a vital link to former ages and brings ancient cultures and history to people today.

Classic art has endured in the works of **Michelangelo, da Vinci, Fra Angelico, Bernini,** and **Raphael.** Ancient manuscripts with meticulous ornate calligraphy are some of the Church's most valuable possessions, such as the ***Book of Kells*** in Dublin. The splendid cathedrals of Germany, France, and Britain, with elaborate architecture and stained-glass windows, tell us important facts of the medieval world. The **Vatican Museums** preserve history and culture of all ages.

Awareness of God in nature in Creation Spirituality has influenced religious art forms today. Banners, plaques, pictures, scenic views, calendars, and greeting cards use people, buildings, scenery, flowers, animals, and events to uplift and inspire. Often these have captions of inspirational or biblical quotes. Although these topics may not be specifically religious, they do inspire, and thus can be listed as religious. It is in the spirit of Teilhard de Chardin who said, "All is sacred. Nothing is profane to him who can see."

Religious stores provide a wide range of religious goods, from the traditional to the modern. Scan the offerings and see the gamut of religious art. Religious goods, however, are not exempt from tawdry commercialism. Entrepreneurs take advantage of any opportunity to pawn their wares. For instance, recall how the pope's image was used

Angelico, Fra   *Dominican monk and Italian painter of important religious works (1387–1455)*

Bernini, Gian Lorenzo   *Italian sculptor of the baroque style with many religious works (1598–1680)*

Book of Kells   *Illuminated Latin manuscript of the four Gospels and related material, produced between the mid-700s and the early 800s in an Irish monastery*

Da Vinci, Leonardo   *Italian Renaissance painter (1452–1519) with many important religious pieces to his credit*

Michelangelo   *Italian sculptor, painter, and architect (1475–1564), responsible for some of the greatest religious art*

Raphael   *Great painter of the Italian Renaissance (1483–1520) with a vast number of religious works to his credit*

Vatican Museums   *Buildings in Vatican City which contain priceless treasures of art from all ages*

on almost anything when he last visited the United States. The height of religious gimmickry has been found outside St. John Lateran's in Rome: hawkers were selling "Lolly-Popes." You guessed it: lollipops with the image of the smiling pope.

While art forms vary, and every person has their own preference, religious art is to inspire. The basic criteria to distinguish between appropriate and inappropriate art, is to ask if it uplifts and inspires and does not stand in the way of devotion.

Sacred Places

The most revered and honored place by Catholics is the church in which the Eucharist is present and where the community gathers for worship. The cemetery, too, is sacred because of belief in the resurrection of the dead and respect paid to the deceased. The Holy Land and Rome are sacred **pilgrimage** sites for Catholics because of their historic and spiritual significance.

Other places, called **shrines,** are sacred, either because a holy person is associated with the place, or because some supernatural event occurred there. Some shrines are so named and designated, such as the **National Shrine of the Immaculate Conception** in Washington, D.C. A crowned shrine is one that the Church accepts as a place where miracles took place, such as **Lourdes** and **Fatima.** A public shrine is one that is authorized by the Church and at which public worship is allowed.

Fatima   *Shrine in Portugal, a place of miracles dating back to the early part of the twentieth century; related to an apparition of Mary*

Lourdes   *Shrine in France, a place of miracles dating back to the latter part of the nineteenth century; related to an apparition of Mary*

National Shrine of the Immaculate Conception   *Important United States shrine in Washington, D.C.*

Pilgrimage   *A prayerful journey to a place of devotion*

Shrine   *A sacred place associated with a holy person or a supernatural occurrence*

Sometimes a place becomes acclaimed because of a sacred event purported to be occurring there. For instance, people swarm to a place where a miraculous image appears or a statue weeps. Often such sites draw curiosity seekers who do not come for devotional reasons. Whenever a supernatural phenomenon is reported, no public worship is allowed unless it is authorized by diocesan officials after careful investigation.

Catholics may set apart a corner in their homes as a private shrine to be used as a center of prayer and devotion.

Sacred Times

From apostolic times, Sunday has been truly the Lord's Day, because Jesus rose from the dead on a Sunday. Catholics observe Sunday by attending liturgy and observing the day with rest and relaxation.

Other holy days are solemnly observed. On these holy days of obligation, Catholics are required to attend Mass. In the United States, there are six:

December 25—Christmas

January 1—Feast of Mary, Mother of God

Forty days after Easter—**Ascension Day**

August 15—Feast of Mary's **Assumption** into Heaven

November 1—All Saints' Day

December 8—Mary's **Immaculate Conception**

Ascension Day   *Feast recalling Jesus' return to the Father forty days after the resurrection, celebrated forty days after Easter*

Assumption, Feast of the   *August 15; recalls Mary's assumption into heaven*

Immaculate Conception, Feast of the   *December 8; recalls the belief that Mary was conceived without sin*

The **Church calendar** is divided into the mysteries of Christ and celebrated in seasons of the **Church year.**

Advent—begins the liturgical year with the first Sunday of Advent and goes to December 24.

Christmas—begins with the vigil of Christmas on December 24 and goes through the Sunday after January 6.

Lent—begins on Ash Wednesday and lasts until the Holy Thursday Mass of the Lord's Supper.

Easter Triduum—begins with the Mass of the Lord's Supper on Holy Thursday and lasts until Easter Sunday.

Easter Season—begins with Easter and lasts for fifty days to Pentecost.

Ordinary Time—begins after the Sunday following January 6 (which is the end of the Christmas season) and lasts through the day before Ash Wednesday. It also begins the day after Pentecost and ends the day before Advent.

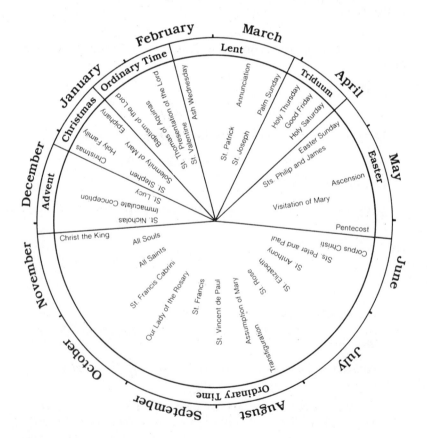

Each season is commemorated with feasts and customs which keep alive the spirit of the celebration. Christmas and Easter are rich in seasonal traditions and cultural customs.

Sacred Persons

Devotion to Mary

After Jesus, no one is beloved by Catholics as is Mary. Devotion to Mary is based on the prominent role she played in the life of Christ, being most closely associated with the acts of redemption. From early days, the Church has recognized the specialness of Mary. Shortly after the divinity of Christ was proclaimed, Mary was proclaimed as the Mother of God, in Ephesus in 431.

Mary is great not only because of her divine maternity, but Mary also exemplifies the perfect human response to God. We can understand this if we reflect on the fact that God has two images of us: what we are and what we can be, our fullest potential. In most of us, these two realities are far apart. But in Mary, they were perfectly integrated. Mary was all that God expected her to be. She is rightfully called, "blessed among women."

Her perfect response and her challenges of faith are the basic keys to her greatness. Mary was truly human, and had to grapple with the reality of what her role was. She doubted, suffered, and struggled as she "pondered these things in her heart." (See Luke 2:19.) The spiritual privileges we believe she was gifted with result from her perfect, total living out of "Let it be done to me. . . ." (Luke 1:38)

Advent   *The liturgical season which begins four Sundays before Christmas*

Church Calendar/Church Year   *The liturgical cycle of seasons and feasts*

Ordinary Time   *Time during the Church year not related to specific feasts: the day after the Sunday after January 6 to the day before Ash Wednesday and the day after Pentecost to the day before Advent*

Since Mary so perfectly embodied God's will and because of her being the mother of Jesus, it is proclaimed as dogma that she was "conceived without sin." This is what we call the Immaculate Conception. We also believe she gave birth without relinquishing her virginity **(Virgin Birth).** Mary was not subject to sin and, therefore, it is proclaimed that she was not allowed to undergo bodily decay in the grave. She was assumed into heaven.

Catholics look up to Mary not so much for these spiritual privileges, but because she is an ideal woman of faith, one to whom we look for guidance. We honor her because she is so fully human, but not beyond our reach. Mary also receives honor because she is the perfect intercessor before the Lord on our behalf.

Over the years, devotion to Mary has assumed many forms. The **Hail Mary,** the most common and familiar of prayers, is basically **Marian theology** in summary. The first part of the prayer is from Luke's account of the annunciation, and the second part, in which we ask her to "pray for us sinners now and at the hour of our death," was added in the Middle Ages when devotion to Mary became popular.

The **rosary,** the prayer said on beads, was popularized by Saint Dominic. In the twelfth century, piety turned to Mary. While the monks recited the psalms in choir, the laity recited the Hail Marys on the beads, while meditating on the mysteries of faith. There are 150 psalms and 150 Hail Marys in the fifteen-decade rosary.

Other devotions to Mary also began in the Middle Ages. The **Angelus bell,** rung at six in the morning, at noon, and at six in the evening was a call to prayer for the monks. Later, it became a threefold summons, and prayers to Mary were recited.

Angelus Bell   *The ringing of the Church bell at 6 A.M., noon, and 6 P.M. to call people to a special prayer in honor of Mary*

Hail Mary   *A common prayer in praise of Mary asking for her intercession*

Marian Theology   *Church teachings and traditions regarding Mary, the Mother of God*

Rosary   *A devotion in honor of Mary and a string of beads used to count the prayers*

Virgin Birth   *The Church dogma or belief that Jesus, the Son of God, was born of only one human parent, Mary, and that she did not lose her virginity*

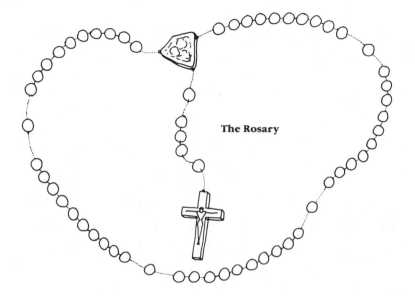

The Rosary

Devotion to Mary in the late nineteenth century and the twentieth century became more pronounced through popular belief in her **apparitions,** especially at Lourdes and Fatima. These devotions fall into the category of private revelation and are not required to be believed as doctrines. However, one cannot ignore or dismiss such occurrences, especially in their role of keeping faith alive.

These devotions, though, ought not to overshadow the scriptural role of Mary in salvation history. There may seem to be a dwindling of showy processions and lengthy novenas, but the Second Vatican Council has restored true devotion by calling Mary, "Mother of the Church." Our theology of Mary today needs to stress her link with salvation events and the ideal woman of faith, who lived the gospel response most perfectly. "Mary shines forth . . . as a sign of sure hope and solace for the pilgrim People of God."[2]

2. Walter M. Abbott, S. J., ed. "Dogmatic Constitution on the Church," *The Documents of Vatican II* (New York: America Press, 1966), p. 95, article 68.

Apparition   *An appearance by Jesus, Mary, saints, or angels to individuals or groups; the Church thoroughly investigates claimed apparitions and approves a few of them that bear the marks of being authentic*

Mary is so special because, in being the Mother of God, she established a unique relationship with all who are joined to Jesus through the Church. Mary, like all mothers, has concern for those with whom her Son is identified.

Devotion to the Saints

In addition to Mary, saints have always played an important role in a Catholic's faith life. We believe the saints are reaping the rewards of a holy life and are now in heaven and have power to intercede for us.

Devotion to the saints is rooted in the Catholic belief in the **Communion of Saints.** Although anyone in heaven is a saint, a saint in the strictest sense of the word is one who is canonized, that is, declared a saint by Church authority as worthy of veneration and honor. Contrary to popular belief, Catholics do not worship saints, although at times exaggerated piety gives that impression. Saints serve as models of Christian virtue, and hence are worthy of honor and imitation.

The cult of saints dates to persecution times, when people considered martyrs as the ideal Christians. Later, possibly a holy villager died, and, when people prayed to him or her, they received special favors. The reputation of this person helping in time of need spread. Shrines were built and people journeyed to his or her grave site or birthplace. Probably this is how devotions to many saints originated.

During the Middle Ages popular piety reached its acme. Saints were acclaimed by the people; legends circulated. There was more emphasis on saints than on the liturgy. Relic trafficking flourished. There was need to control the multiplication of saints. The process of **canonization** was begun in the twelfth century, but laws governing the making of a saint were not enforced seriously until after the Reformation.

Canonization   *The official Church process by which a person is declared a saint of the Catholic Church*

Communion of Saints   *The spiritual union among the saints in heaven, the souls in purgatory, and the faithful on earth*

Canonization today is regulated by the **Sacred Congregation for the Causes of Saints.** After the case is made that the person led a holy life and that he or she ought to be a saint, the cause is introduced by diocesan officials. After much preliminary research concerning one's holiness, a person is declared venerable.

After further research into the person's life and miracles, a person may be **beatified** and declared blessed. This entitles them to be venerated in a certain area or in the religious community to which they belonged.

The entire commission studying the case is on constant lookout for any reason which inhibits the cause from proceeding. They do more extensive research, and then a commission of bishops and cardinals may present the cause to the pope, who formally, in a **Bull of Canonization,** proclaims the person a saint. The saint may now be publicly honored, have churches named after him or her, and be assigned a liturgical feast.

The process of canonization is lengthy, complex, and expensive. Numerous cases are pending, and many others are dropped while in process. Yet canonizations continue. Pope John Paul II has canonized numerous saints. Because the process is so involved, there are many true saints who remain unnamed and anonymous.

In order to keep the cult of saints in proper perspective, in 1969, the Church removed about two hundred names from the official hagiography (list of saints) and the liturgical calendar. It was not known if these saints actually lived or if legends grew from unhistorical sources. Since there was no definite historical data, their official status was dropped. However, some still remain popular, like Saint Christopher, whose image graces the dashboard of cars, the patron of travelers.

Beatification *One of the official steps in the canonization process; the person who is beatified is called "Blessed"*

Bull of Canonization *Official proclamation that a person is a saint*

Sacred Congregation for the Causes of Saints *The office in the Vatican that investigates the lives of people to be declared saints and regulates the process*

Some saints are remembered for certain causes. Saint Anthony is the patron of lost objects; **Saint Jude,** of impossible cases. On the feast of **Saint Blaise,** February 3, Catholics get their throats blessed, because Blaise was supposed to have cured a throat ailment. On the feast of Saint Francis on October 4, animals are blessed, because Francis loved all nature. Many Catholics have favorite saints to whom they pray. Perhaps a favor was received, or one was named after a certain saint, or one just feels attracted to the virtues and life of a saint. However, devotion to saints is one's personal choice and does not fall under Catholic doctrine.

Some saints' popularity extends into the secular realm. Valentine's Day, St. Patrick's Day, and Christmas are connected with saints: **Saint Valentine,** a bishop in the early Church; **Saint Patrick,** who converted Ireland; and **Saint Nicholas** (Santa Claus), a bishop of Myra who doled out gifts and presents to the needy.

Relics, that is, any object directly connected with a saint, are not holy in themselves, but are revered by Catholics because of their link with the saint. The tradition started when the early Christians gathered fragments of bones and ashes of the martyrs and placed them in altars. The custom of celebrating Mass at an altar in which a relic of a saint is placed is an ancient tradition, which at one time was mandatory. In our day of movable altars, the custom is not essential. Relics are not to be sold, and the relic documentation is regulated by the same congregation as for saints.

Relic   *Any part of the bodily remains of a saint; items connected to the saint's life, such as clothing*

Saint Blaise   *The saint on whose feast day, February 3, Catholics may participate in the sacramental blessing of throats*

Saint Jude   *An apostle, also known as Thaddeus, regarded as the patron of hopeless causes*

Saint Nicholas   *A bishop of Myra known for his charity, giving rise to the story of Santa Claus*

Saint Patrick   *The saint traditionally considered responsible for the conversion of Ireland; his feast day, March 17, is celebrated by Irish everywhere*

Saint Valentine   *The saint whose feast day has become the secular celebration of Valentine's Day, February 14*

While devotion to the saints is encouraged and beneficial to one's spirituality, it needs to be balanced and kept secondary to the worship of God. Vatican II warns against "abuses, excesses, or defects which may have crept in here and there, and to restore all things to a more ample praise of Christ and of God. The authentic cult of the saints consists not so much in the multiplying of external acts, but rather in the intensity of our active love."[3]

Devotions to the saints and the use of sacramentals are aids and accessories to one's faith. They are the side dishes; the entrée is worship of God through Christ in liturgy and sacraments. Sacramentals, devotions, and saints lead us to a greater awareness of Jesus in our midst. Their presence in our homes is a constant reminder of Jesus who said, "I am with you always." (Matthew 28:20)

3. Walter M. Abbott, S. J., ed. "Dogmatic Constitution on the Church," *The Documents of Vatican II* (New York: America Press, 1966), p. 84, article 51.

IX

How Does a Catholic Live as a Morally Responsible Person?

Morality—Love—Sin—Original Sin—Fundamental Option—Capital Sins—Ten Commandments—Hell—Precepts of the Church—Code of Canon Law—Sermon on the Mount—Beatitudes—Corporal Works of Mercy—Spiritual Works of Mercy—Gifts of the Spirit—Fruits of the Spirit

Introduction

If any aspect of Catholic teaching has shifted significantly, it is in the area of morality. Throughout the ages, morality has evolved from the simple Law of Love to a complex code of regulated behavior.

But Vatican II shifted from a mechanical form of morality to a vibrant, active, responsible living of Christian values. This change from a staid morality to a creative morality probably was one of the most necessary shifts in attitude, and yet it is possibly the most misunderstood. Catholics have been ruffled and uncertain at the "new" morality. Some have welcomed the change gracefully; others wish they could, but are still caught in the traditional mode of thought. Still others are totally against the change.

In this chapter, we clarify this new approach by looking at morality attitudes through the ages. We reflect on what morality and the formation of a right conscience mean today. Law, sin, and other concepts are examined in the light of contemporary theology.

Development of Moral Laws

For the early Christians, morality was synonymous with commitment to Christ. Regulations were minimal. Their **love** and commitment to Jesus showed in their care and concern for each other. "The community of believers were of one heart and one mind. None of them ever claimed anything as his own." (Acts 4:32) Christ had made a difference in their lives, and it showed in how they lived the "Way."

As Christianity spread and became more prevalent, all types of peoples were converted. Stipulations were drawn up because the Christian life was a radical conversion from their former ways. Gradually, due to the influences of Greek thought on theology, soul and body were seen as opposing. Flesh and material world concerns were considered detrimental to one's salvation. Thus an unhealthy, obsessive concern about sin resulted in greatly diminishing, if not eradicating, the emphasis on goodness and the living out of gospel values.

Norms of morality became standard and gelled into a specific legal code in the Middle Ages, especially with the Fourth Lateran Council. Spirituality became more preoccupied with the afterlife and salvation than with the present life. Spiritual favors were purchased; penance for sin was done by proxies. Taking part in the Crusades was seen as a guarantee of salvation.

Love *Charity and concern for self, others, and God*

By the time of the Reformation, moral abuses were widespread. The Council of Trent, in seeking to balance and rid the Church of abuses, stepped in with exacting firmness. Every aspect of Catholic living was regulated and standardized. Morality was no exception. Catholics knew exactly what was expected, for everything was detailed.

To live a moral life was to obey the rules set up by the Council. Law, therefore, became the supreme value. Every iota of a person's actions became a legal issue. One's religiosity was gauged by one's avoidance of sin. A confession-oriented approach resulted in an "Is-it-a-sin" mentality. The clergy acted as judges and were aided by lists of sins with accompanying penances. Moral life involved obeying a set of laws. The Commandments were negatively phrased deterrents.

One's growth in holiness was determined by how well one kept the Commandments. A common perception was that, if one did not break the Commandments, he or she was moral. If a person gave in and committed sin, all one had to do was go to confession, and sin was forgiven. If one did not go to confession, one "in the state of mortal sin" at the time of death would go to hell. Such an attitude spawned a fear and a negative spirituality. In this closed, narrow morality, there was rarely a mention of gospel values.

Sad to say, this is the moral climate in which Catholics before Vatican II grew up. "To avoid sin" was emphasized more than "to do good." Vatican II, in seeking to recapture authentic gospel values and a commitment-oriented morality, had to approach the Church's understanding of moral living in a revolutionary manner. No longer do old thought patterns of static morality aid one in living in the spirit of Vatican II.

In order to grasp and appreciate the values of reform and renewal, one needs to forget the former and forge ahead into a renewed morality which considers positive values and goodness. Because the pre-Vatican II morality has been so deeply imbedded in the Catholic psyche, the old approach to morality has been hard to uproot and transplant with fresh insights from contemporary theological developments.

Morality in the Spirit of Vatican II

When we look at morality in the spirit of Vatican II, we must understand the shifts of emphasis which occurred. The Church invented no "new" morality in itself, but rather shifted the emphasis, so that we speak of a new approach. Let us examine some of those shifts and how they affect the way we look at our morality.

Jesus, in dying and rising from the dead, has bestowed on the world a redeeming quality. The world was created good. The world, created in goodness and redeemed, has been transformed and is a sanctifying agent. It aids us to holiness. Therefore, the world is not to be shunned and avoided. The true Christian attempts to make Christ's love visible in the world by a life of love.

Moral living today involves doing one's share to redeem the world by infusing into it as much love as we can. For the Catholic of today who wishes to live in the spirit of Vatican II, love is the highest moral value, not law. Father Bernard Häring, a noted moral theologian has captured the essence of Vatican II in many of his writings. "Morality," he explains, "is fidelity to the human vocation of love."

This leads to another shift of emphasis. Vatican II considers freedom to be one of humanity's greatest endowments. Human persons are gifted by the Creator with the capacity to create "a new heaven and a new earth." Therefore, one's well-formed conscience is seen as the ultimate norm of morality. People need to develop a responsible conscience which bases decisions on gospel values and the spirit of Christ.

To achieve a formed, as well as an informed, conscience, one must ask oneself: Is this action making me a better person? Is this action or attitude in accord with the spirit of Jesus? Is this in accord with the teachings of the Church? Is love my underlying motive?

This requires a reordering of priorities. If one is concerned about the most loving mode of behavior, then one can overcome selfishness and think first of others. Apathy towards the needs of others may be as morally wrong as a specific sinful action.

This new approach to morality is not less challenging or demanding. In fact, it is more exacting. The responsibility for goodness lies within oneself. Mature responses demand a harsh, straightforward honesty. To be morally alive with goodness and values, one must be able to look at one's actions according to their harmony with God's plan for the world.

New understandings of words have also aided us to grasp the true meaning of this moral teaching in the mind of the Church today. We do not speak of freedom in the sense of license and do-as-you-please thinking. Rather, true freedom of spirit lies in knowing what is expected of one as a responsible moral person at this point in one's life. Responsibility implies that one knows one's duties and wills to act accordingly.

With an authentic morality, a person bases decisions and patterns of behavior on a deeper understanding of the dignity and call of human persons to live lives which extend Christ's love and compassion in the world. This intensifies the presence of goodness.

The morality of today does not negate absolute moral principles, but considers them essential foundations on which to base moral decisions. The ideas of sin, law, and hell are still part of Catholic theology, but with a changed perspective. Let us examine these in the light of the teachings of Vatican II.

What Is Sin?

Sin still is rampant and is as new and fresh as this morning's news. Its intensity is seen all around. Sin is not an aggregate of individual bad acts, nor is it single isolated violations of a law. Sin does not merely involve the committing of one action, being sorry for it, going to confession, and forgetting its effects.

Sin results from a pattern of behavior we have allowed to develop in our lives. We are prone to be attracted to less than perfect actions due to the innate evil tendency within us we call **original sin.** *Sinfulness* is an appropriate term to use for the propensity to do wrong. Sinfulness becomes sin by repetition. It is like one who has a glass filled over and over. But it is the one swig which makes one drunk. The drunkenness has been building up. Sinfulness rests on inner motivations and tendencies and escalates into a pattern of wrongdoing.

Theologians call this habit of tending toward sin or away from it, our **fundamental option.** It is an underlying current pulling us toward and deeper into a basic pattern of behavior, oriented toward God or away from God. One does not fall into sin. You can say one chooses it through one's fundamental option.

Fundamental Option   *The life choice a person makes toward or away from God; this life choice is reinforced by a pattern of behavior*

Original Sin   *The result of the sin of our first parents which affects all people in its consequences*

So what about the notion of mortal and venial sin? In former days, we put sin into convenient boxes and labeled them serious or not so serious. Today, we take into account other factors when judging the morality of actions. Mortal sin exists and is the total rejection of God. But, in deciding the seriousness, many subjective factors come into play. Two people do the same action. For one, it is morally acceptable; for the other, it may be a serious sin. For example, the sex act between a married couple can be a spiritual act of love; whereas, the same action between a couple not married to each other is not morally acceptable. The degree of rightness or wrongness depends on the will, motivation, knowledge, and consent.

The main sources or roots of sin are called the **capital sins.** They are: pride, covetousness, lust, anger, gluttony, envy, and sloth. These evil roots are evident also in the social structures of the world. "All institutions—churches, corporations, governments—fall short of stated goals. They have within them a kind of inertia which tugs away from the good that they set out as their end."[1]

The Concept of Law in Vatican II Thought

Laws are necessary in any organization in order to preserve harmony and peace. The basic law to which everyone is subject is the **Natural Law,** which can be known by human reason. Humans realize what basic goodness demands of them.

---

1. Lawrence Cunningham. *The Catholic Faith: An Introduction* (New York: Paulist Press, 1987), p. 118.

Capital Sins   *The seven main sources or roots of sin: pride, covetousness, lust, anger, gluttony, envy, and sloth*

Natural Law   *The laws which govern the nature of things; the natural moral law refers to proper human action by people*

The Ten Commandments, considered the Divine Positive Law, because they were revealed by God, are concerned with people's basic relationships to God and to neighbor. Although they are presented in negative terms, "Thou shalt not . . .," their essence is concerned with positive values. Moral education today needs to inculcate the positive attitudes, rather than focus on the prohibitions.

The Concept of Hell in Vatican II Thought

Despite rumors to the contrary, **hell** is still a doctrine in Catholic theology. One who purposely rejects God chooses not to enjoy an eternity of friendship with the Lord. This is the basic notion of hell—cutting oneself off from God.

The existence of hell or separation from God is very real. However, what form hell assumes or in what manner a damned person will suffer, is open to debate. No one has come back and given the temperature of the eternal fire. And no human can judge whether another is damned. Theologians suggest that hell be seen as a state of total rejection of God. Like heaven, it is not a place and is not subject to time.

In grappling with the issue of hell, one needs to remember that it is an issue which remains in the realm of mystery, a truth not yet entirely revealed.

Church Law— Precepts of the Church

In addition to God's law, there are six **Precepts of the Church** or moral obligations of Catholics. These laws act as guidelines and state what the minimum requirements are for Catholics

Hell   *The state of eternal rejection of God*

Precepts of the Church   *Six Church laws governing Catholics*

in order to be considered active participants in the life of the Church. These basic laws are:

- *To participate in Mass on Sundays and holy days*

- *To fast and abstain on days appointed*—Fast days are Ash Wednesday and Good Friday, when one full meal is allowed. Ash Wednesday and the Fridays of Lent are days of abstinence when no meat is allowed.

- *To confess once a year if one is in serious sin*

- *To receive Communion at least once a year* (between the first Sunday of Lent and Trinity Sunday)

- *To obey the laws concerning marriage*

- *To support the Church*

- *To join in the missionary spirit of the Church* (United States addition)

Code of Canon Law

The Code of Canon Law is the official body of legislation which governs the entire structure of ecclesial discipline. The revised Code, issued in 1983, replaces the older Code, set up in 1918. The reforms of Vatican II have been implemented in the present Code of Canon Law.

Although ordinary Catholics need not be concerned with the Code directly, the norms and rules affect the juridical aspects of Catholic life. The 1752 canons consider specific issues divided into seven books: General Norms, The People of God, The Teaching Office of the Church, The Sanctifying Office of the Church, The Temporal Goods of the Church, Sanctions in the Church, and Processes. The Code of Canon Law primarily deals with matters which direct the carrying out of Church norms and rules.

Other Moral Considerations for Catholics

In carrying out one's responsibilities, a Catholic cannot ignore the demands and laws of the sociopolitical realm. As a citizen, one obeys the regulations of civic authority as well as policies established in the workplace.

The morality of today is not without its challenges. Advances in science and technology present moral dilemmas that did not exist in previous generations. Theologians and scientists need to work together to explore issues concerning the basic dignity and right to life. There are genetic issues concerning surrogate motherhood, test-tube babies, and genetic engineering. Medical issues dealing with transplants, life-support systems, and dying with dignity need to be looked at from a moral perspective. Other areas of moral consideration include capital punishment, nuclear warfare, AIDS, and political structures.

Catholics need to form an authentic conscience which embraces more than their own actions. One needs to take a stand on issues that affect the well-being of others. Therefore, a moral person gets involved in social justice interests. This requires fortitude and integrity. One who is moral is completely honest in all business dealings, gives everyone their due, and is governed by the Law of Love.

When one is caught in the web of conflict, torn between alternatives, and not knowing which course to pursue, one must weigh the issue responsibly, pray, and decide sincerely what is the most moral path to follow. A rightly-formed conscience can rest peacefully with decisions.

All one's actions need to be governed by the great commandment: "You shall love the Lord your God with all your heart, with all your soul, with all your mind, and all your strength." (Mark 12:30, Deuteronomy 6:5) Likewise, "Love your neighbor as yourself." On these precepts rests the whole moral law. Love motivates one toward the good.

Practical, everyday situations which demand a moral decision require that a person be able to establish priorities. It would hardly be considered morally plausible for one to volunteer many hours at a soup kitchen and neglect one's family. Extra charity may give one greater satisfaction, but devotion to one's duty and prime obligation needs to take precedence. Neither does one need to develop a messiah complex. One is not bound to assist every needy person who comes across one's path.

Moral training and education must be based on the values of Jesus as found in the Scriptures. The **Sermon on the Mount** and the **Beatitudes,** as found in Matthew (chapters 5–7) and Luke (chapter 6), challenge us to a radical conversion and way of life according to the mind of Christ. This spirit is spelled out further in the Corporal and Spiritual Works of Mercy.

The **Corporal Works of Mercy** are: to feed the hungry, to give drink to the thirsty, to clothe the naked, to visit the imprisoned, to shelter the homeless, to visit the sick, and to bury the dead. The **Spiritual Works of Mercy** are: to admonish the sinner, to instruct the ignorant, to counsel the doubtful, to comfort the sorrowful, to bear wrongs patiently, to forgive injuries and hurts, and to pray for the living and the dead. If we examine these and live them, we will be adhering to most of the requirements for Christian living in our actions.

Living the moral life also includes heeding the work of the Spirit within us, who graces us with spiritual strength. Therefore, in our consideration of morality, we cannot overlook the virtues and habits one develops by responding to the Spirit. In theological language, we have called these qualities the Fruits and Gifts of the Spirit. These lie at the base of our morality and show forth in our actions. They are open to all.

The **Gifts of the Spirit,** as mentioned in Isaiah 11:2–3, are: wisdom, understanding, counsel, fortitude, knowledge, piety, and fear of the Lord. Saint Paul speaks of the **Fruits of the Spirit** in Galatians 5:22–23. He upholds the goodness of virtue as opposed to a life of sin. The twelve Fruits of the Spirit include: charity, joy, peace,

Beatitudes   *A list of blessings included in the Sermon on the Mount in Matthew's Gospel, with variations in Luke's Gospel*

Corporal Works of Mercy   *Seven charitable works encouraged by the Church*

Fruits of the Spirit   *Twelve virtues related to the work of the Holy Spirit in people*

Gifts of the Spirit   *Seven virtues related to the work of the Holy Spirit in people*

Sermon on the Mount   *Chapters 5–7 of Matthew's Gospel, which includes many of Jesus' teachings*

Spiritual Works of Mercy   *Seven spiritual charitable works encouraged by the Church*

patience, kindness, goodness, long-suffering, mildness, faith, modesty, continence, and chastity. These are specifically mentioned because it would be a beneficial practice, when one examines one's conscience, to consider how one includes the exercise of positive good habits, instead of focusing solely on the negative vices.

Morality as Creative Goodness

To live a moral life is not just to avoid sin or evil. We ought not live by an avoidance, negative morality, but by a positive, dynamic, creative morality. The moral person asks the question, "What *can* I do?" rather than "What *must* I do?"

Ordinary, daily actions and decisions do not revolve around the choice between vice and virtue. Most of our routine deeds involve choices between the good or the better. They are not mainly decisions of right or wrong, allowed or forbidden.

There is more to life than fulfilling obligations. A mother who does the minimum of feeding and clothing her child and does nothing more, can hardly be considered living up to her moral responsibilities. The amount of our creative goodness outweighs the good we must do. Duty is the least we can do in a situation.

Each one can create a moral climate by making the world a better place and by doing one's best in one's situation. To diffuse virtue and goodness as much as possible in one's environment and world is living the moral life intensely and fully. We can, therefore, create our own level of goodness. We can opt for the barest minimum or do our best in every situation. It is putting one's heart into one's work; it is doing the most loving thing in every instance. Think what a wonderful world it would be if each person would try to do the most loving actions at all times. Imagine if all would diffuse as much as possible of Christ's loving presence.

God left for people a task for moral creativity at creation, "to cultivate and care for" the earth. (Genesis 2:15) God referred not only to ecology, but to the fact that humanity is called to make the world a fully human place, with moral goodness diffused through the moral choices of people.

To be baptized and to live the Catholic faith in the spirit of Vatican II is to live the challenge of Christ in a morally responsible way. It is to live a moral life through love, not coercion.

One who heeds the voice of Christ makes a difference in the world. Of a Catholic and any Christian who follows Christ in a morality of love and responsibility, it can be said, "You are the salt of the earth. . . . You are the light of the world." (Matthew 5:13, 14) A moral Christian aches and feels pain in the sufferings of others. Social injustices are decried, and the rights of the oppressed are upheld.

The morality of Vatican II calls us to "preserve a view of the whole human person, a view in which the values of intellect, will, conscience, and fraternity are pre-eminent. These values are all rooted in God the Creator and have been wonderfully restored and elevated in Christ."[2] Such a responsible attitude can effect a change which brings Christ's presence more dynamically into the world. The mission of the Church is to be a sign, to transform the world, and to evoke its redeeming qualities. The way to show forth the presence of God within the world is with a morality built on love and Christ's teachings.

---

2. Walter M. Abbott, S. J., ed. "Pastoral Constitution on the Church in the Modern World," *The Documents of Vatican II* (New York: America Press, 1966), p. 267, article 61.

X

Why and How Do Catholics Pray?

Spirituality—Prayer—Charismatic Prayer—Jesus Prayer—Contemplation—Centering Prayer—Retreats

Introduction

Catholics are called to a community of faith which observes traditions, rituals, and ceremonies in company with others. But there is another side to Catholic living without which the practice of religion would not make sense. One needs to develop an intimate, personal, one-to-one friendship with Christ. Responding to and experiencing Christ on a personal level is what we can call one's spirituality. Each person responds to Christ in life as no one else ever has or will. One's personal life of prayer grows and develops as one becomes more attuned to the Lord working in one's unique situations.

In this chapter, we look at how a Catholic can develop this sense of God through a deep spirituality and prayer life. We first explore the meaning of a personal spirituality. We offer suggestions of the various ways a person can pray. We conclude with practical suggestions on how one can improve and grow in knowledge and experience of the Lord.

Personal Spirituality

Each person is called into existence as someone special. "I have called you by name: you are mine," we read in Isaiah 43:1. Through baptism, a Christian is initiated into a special relationship with Christ. The Church leads and guides, but each person needs to develop a close friendship with Jesus, to know him intimately.

Catholics, too, are called to a deeper life of union with God. It is not accomplished solely by going through the motions of rituals and ceremonies. We respond to God's love on a personal level by tapping the resources of God within our inner souls.

To live the Catholic faith fully is to make the reality of God part of our lives. In *Dynamics of Faith,* Paul Tillich calls this personal faith a "movement from seizing truths about God, to being seized by the truth of God."[1] Unless the presence of Christ is felt as a personal reality in the heart, Catholic practices or any outward manifestation of faith is merely a facade. Father Leonard Foley notes, "If our lives are faith-filled, they are prayer. If our prayer is genuine, our life is faith-filled."[2]

Mister God, This Is Anna, a delightful little book, is a laugh-and-cry tale of a young man who befriends a lonely waif, Anna. She has an intimate relationship with God. "People . . . when they go to church . . . measure Mister God from the outside." They need to get inside and measure Mister God.[3]

This kind of faith requires familiarity with God on a personal level. It means living on a two-dimensional plane. People are body and soul, and both need to be developed if one is to be fully human.

There is more to life than VCRs, the IRS, RVs, Social Security, taxes, lotteries, or cruises. Although there are many demands on modern humans, meaningful existence is more important and more satisfying than a merely pleasurable existence. We are called to live as humanly as possible. If we are totally honest, this involves living a life in the Spirit. It is making God a very real part of daily life.

Jesus does not relegate his grace to Church activities only. He follows us into the marketplace, into our homes, into our work. To

---

1. Paul Tillich, *Dynamics of Faith* (New York: Harper and Row).

2. Leonard Foley, O.F.M., *Believing in Jesus* (Cincinnati: St. Anthony Messenger Press, 1985), p. 155.

3. Fynn, *Mister God, This Is Anna* (New York: Holt, Rinehart, and Winston, 1974), p. 85.

live spiritually is to take notice, to wonder, and to see the hand of God splashed all over the world. We become God-discoverers in our lives by discovering the near-range of the Lord working with us. He does not necessarily come in a flamboyant style, but to everyone in a unique way. It may be that God is seen and experienced in a sunset, snowfall, smile, or symphony. God breaks into our lives wherever we are, if we are open to His revelations.

One young mother related that she did not know what was wrong with her. As she went about her daily chores, she had an ongoing conversation with God. She thought perhaps she was acting abnormal. After discussing her life, attitudes, and other aspects of her faith, the listener came to realize that she had achieved a deep level of true contemplative prayer and genuine spirituality.

Spirituality such as this is not for a select few. Everyone is called to a deeper relationship with God. We need to respond to God's presence with a vibrant, dynamic faith. This interplay of God calling people to an intimate friendship and people responding with a spiritual outlook has been called grace, which is the relationship between humans and their Creator.

We meet God on our own wavelength according to our unique individuality. People, in their personal quest for God, search as solitary beings. "No one can prescribe for man his pact with the Infinite."[4]

God is someone whose presence overwhelms. His magnitude makes us serene. God baffles, upsets, makes us wonder and marvel. He haunts more than He dominates. He pursues people and He loves. His continual elusiveness makes us feel small, humble, and insignificant. Yet, He attracts us and also mystifies us. When we think we have grasped His ways, we are surprised into other discoveries. God's presence in our lives comes at unexpected moments. Sometimes He is soft and serene; other times He barges in with dramatic savvy.

The Divine in our lives is the One we need. He has no need of us, yet our response to His love is what makes us truly human. We have attempted to understand God more by labeling Him. But we need to encounter Him more meaningfully. We need to be attuned to the modes in which He manifests Himself to us. Like all relationships, our attempts to become more intimate with the Lord cannot be prescribed nor measured. Spirituality is a process which grows. There is an ebb and flow. At times, God may seem so near; at other times, we may wonder if He exists.

---

4. Gordon Allport, *The Individual and His Religion* (New York: Macmillan, 1967).

But a life of union and awareness of God is not a human luxury. It is part of our human condition. Saint Augustine notes, "Thou hast made us for thyself, O Lord, and our hearts are restless until they rest in Thee." We are made by God and our ultimate destiny is God. We come from God in order to come to God. Sometimes we get so caught up in concern for rules and rituals that this personal aspect of religion is overlooked. With renewal and our awareness of the working of the Spirit in our Church today, Catholics are finding fresh vitality in the various movements and opportunities for personal, spiritual growth. In relating to Christ as a personal friend, we can say along with Dag Hammarskjöld, "At some moment I did answer *Yes* to Someone—or Something—and from that hour I was certain that existence is meaningful and that, therefore, my life, in self-surrender, had a goal."[5]

Role and Types of Prayer in One's Personal Spirituality

To become intimate with God is to develop a life of prayer, as part of daily living. "Prayer," says Abraham Heschel, "is the humble answer to the inconceivable surprise of living."

Prayer needs to be seen as part of the rhythm of day-by-day experiences. It is grasping the prayerful moments and being united in love with God. One makes use of the times in which one is moved to enlarge oneself and see life in its deeper dimensions. One prays when one needs to expand oneself and relate to a greater being than oneself. And so I pray when I see an Olympic skater fall in a competition; I pray at the sight of a gorgeous sunset; I pray when I hear an ambulance shrieking to an emergency.

Prayer happens when one opens oneself to the Divine realities in life. Prayer releases inner tensions and provides a person with solace in time of distress. Everyone can pray. No previous experience is required, although one becomes more adept and comfortable with practice. Prayer comes naturally because people recognize that there are some things in life over which we have no control. Witness the atmosphere in an emergency room. Behind the flurry of doctors and nurses to save lives, there are the silent sentinels who await news of the condition of a loved one. Everyone can become a fervent "prayer." Our human limits exhausted, we open to Divine help and assistance.

---

5. Dag Hammarskjöld, *Markings* (New York: Alfred A. Knopf, 1964), p. 205.

Prayer is as varied as human creativity. In order to communicate meaningfully with God, we adopt a prayer style with which we feel at ease and one which aids toward deeper spirituality. Catholics have been accustomed to praying in union with others, reciting prayers, and using prayerbooks. In expanding our spiritual horizons, it is most helpful to consider a variety of prayer forms. Although we prefer one type over another as matter of choice, it is beneficial to be open to new insights and various methods.

Let us examine some of the methods one can utilize in prayer. If some are new, it would be profitable to experiment and be creative in our relationship with God, just as we are in human relationships.

Traditional

Catholics are familiar with traditional prayers, from saying the rosary together to reciting the Creed. The recital of prayers as such can lead to routine. One can be creative by praying the prayers in a slow deliberate way. Mull over each phrase, savor it, meditate on its deeper meanings. One may be surprised at the insights received. It is a leisurely contemplation of what we pray.

One may also achieve a quieting and serenity by reciting prayers. An example of this is a mantra. As it is repeated over and over, a spiritual calm results. The rosary, said devoutly, effects a peace and union with God.

Communal

When Catholics join in prayer with others, the prayer is called "communal." This type is used in saying the rosary, offering novena prayers, and in praying the Divine Office. Although this latter form of prayer has been used by priests and religious for centuries, since Vatican II the Liturgy of the Hours is being prayed by many of the laity as well, either in private or with others.

Shared Prayer

Jesus said that where two or three were gathered in his name, he is in their midst. It is an enriching experience when people join together to share prayer concerns. The group, in praying with each other and listening to each one expressing his or her prayer, supports each other. This sharing in common of one's prayerful concerns leads to fresh insights about how the Lord works in everyone's life and the realization that we all share the same limitations and needs.

With shared prayer groups becoming more common, many people need to overcome their basic shyness. The spontaneous sharing may aid in a closer friendship with Christ as well as with the community.

Charismatic Prayer

With the renewal of spirituality has come a deeper realization of the Spirit at work in the world today. The charismatic movement focuses on the Holy Spirit alive and active. Charismatic prayer is characterized by praise and honor of God in joyful proclamations. It is dynamic and enthusiastic in its expression. Someone who prefers quiet prayer may find charismatic prayer too loud.

"The Spirit lives and we gladly proclaim it" is the clarion call of charismatic prayer. The spirit of the early Christians has been recaptured and the sometimes stolid coldness of prayer and ritual is replaced by a living in the Spirit.

Instant Spontaneous Prayer

We are a people of instants. Commodities all cater to our craving for instant gratification. Prayer, too, can be an instant. These are short and spontaneous on-the-spot prayers. We can repeat one over and over, such as the **Jesus Prayer.** It is a prayer which has been used by Eastern Christians for many years. "Lord, Jesus, be merciful to me, a sinner" was seen as a way to keep in constant touch with God.

One need not be so formal. One can creatively use any thought which helps one to be reflective. While at work, at leisure, or at home, one can be united to the Lord by sending up short prayer thoughts. "Jesus, I need you now. Help me to decide what's best," can be a meaningful prayer.

One can use imagination, too, in one's prayers. We often were led to believe that this is not proper. For instance, try Alphabet Prayers. Ask the Lord for special qualities, alphabetically. Use this method in praying for world needs, for others, and for one's own intentions.

Creativity involves a freedom. You need to feel so at ease with the Lord that He is part of every life situation you encounter. Just as

Jesus Prayer   *A common Eastern Rite prayer: Lord, Jesus, be merciful to me, a sinner*

one deeply in love with another does not let too many moments go by without associating with that person in spirit, so also, when one lives in union with God, one's day is flavored with a spiritual dimension. With God at one's side, life is seen with a divine perspective. "God and I are a majority," as Saint Teresa of Avila said and lived out.

Creative Prayer

As one becomes familiar with Christ and closer as a friend, one becomes attuned to God's presence everywhere. The world reminds one of God, and so one can pray at the seashore, in the mountains, on a crowded subway, in one's room, or in church.

All we experience in life can point to a spiritual significance. Such an approach to life requires that we be reflective creatures, and see deeper meanings in life's mundane realities. For instance, how can you be creatively spiritual while sipping coffee from your favorite mug? Think of the security we find in our mug. We hold on to it and are devastated if it slips from our hands and shatters in pieces. Life is "holding on" and "letting go." We all need security and find it in many ways. As one becomes reflective, other deeper insights come, if only we sit still long enough to allow God some space in our daily lives.

God speaks loudly in nature, splattered in variegated colors and splendor in the sky, in flowers, in all that is around us. The person who prays creatively can use all avenues as raw material for prayer. He can find God in a soul-stirring episode on TV, in a popular song, and in the ordinary. God is everywhere, if only we look. God comes amid the bustle of the marketplace or in silence. Music has a haunting quality which makes Divinity seem near. Who can listen to "Moonlight Sonata" without being inspired? Creative prayer is seen in poignant quotes on refrigerator doors or on desk plaques. One needs to have reminders to provide instant inspiration.

If we have been accustomed to pigeon-hole religion from daily life, such an approach to prayer may be unfamiliar. But once one begins seeing God in this light, there will be no end to the surprises and insights.

Peak Experiences

There are times when the Lord breaks into our lives with the suddenness and violence of a summer monsoon. This peak experience is a moment when one is totally at one with the Lord. It may be called a born-again experience.

This enthusiastic and powerful spiritual energy is found in charismatic gatherings, but also in one's personal life. It may come at those special moments: at the birth of a child; at a stirring religious ceremony, like Christmas Midnight Mass; or at one's quiet prayer time. All reality blends perfectly. We feel so at one with everything and everyone around us.

Since one cannot travel through life on mountain peaks, these experiences come only rarely. Peak experiences cannot be programmed, nor can they be repeated. They are God's special gifts, given when God's wisdom deems.

Prayer of Quiet—Contemplation

When we speak of prayer, we usually think of our efforts to reach God. True, when we speak, God listens. But prayer is reciprocal. When God speaks, we must listen. We are often too caught up in daily concerns, and prayer is an active exercise, something done, words spoken, rituals performed.

"Be still and know that I am God," the psalmist advises. It is like the quiet sustained relationship of two people who have spent a lifetime together and have grown old in love. Time together is not spent in endless babble, but in being present to each other. They may pass an entire evening and not say a word. They do not need to. They are dynamically present to each other. There are no words, only love.

This is the prayer of quiet. We are present to the Lord, basking in the warmth of His love, no words, no favors, no action, just quiet **contemplation.** Such a mode is not reserved for contemplatives, but is a way that everyone can strive to attain. It requires discipline and effort. It takes time and patience. It is the way an old friend prayed. "I say nothing. I look at God and He looks back at me."

We are always too harried and busy to take time to sit perfectly still. We plan; we regulate. But if we give God our time, He will give us a glimpse of His life. Such a method is not beyond our reach. In fact, people may be praying this way and not even realize it.

Today, this type of prayer is being practiced in **centering prayer.** By basking in the presence of God, giving time without any

Centering Prayer   *A type of contemplation in which the person directs all of his or her energy inward*

Contemplation   *The prayer of quiet, an intimate being-with the Lord*

words, one focuses on one word or thought to assist in centering. Deep insights and a reflective attitude enable one to experience peace and serenity.

Other Spiritual Means in Personal Spirituality

Anyone who takes his or her relationship with God seriously soon realizes that prayer is not merely a spontaneous, easily-attained practice. It requires a commitment in faith and fidelity. One needs to prepare.

Ways which make prayer easier include a deeper effort to use the aids and helps available. Daily or weekday Mass hones one's spiritual sense. Through spiritual reading one shares in the insights of others who take God seriously. There are many books which assist one in striving to know God better. One also will take advantage of spiritual retreats in a group, such as the **Cursillo, Marriage Encounters,** or parish renewal retreats. Private retreats enable one to focus on one's spiritual life in an intense way. No longer the monopoly of religious communities, retreats for laity are becoming more common. Spiritual direction aids one to a deeper relationship with God. This is the aim of our baptismal commitment.

We all need to discover: "To fall in love with God is the greatest romance—to seek God is the greatest adventure—and to find God is the highest human achievement," as Saint Augustine experienced.

Cursillo *A religious experience weekend begun in Spain whose goal is to change the world by remaking it according to the mind of Christ*

Marriage Encounter *A weekend religious experience for married couples which aims to make good marriages better*

XI

What Do Catholics Believe?

**Faith—Belief—Trinity—Tradition—
Deposit of Faith—Dogma—Doctrine—
Nicene Creed—Kerygma—Apostles'
Creed—Council of Trent—Catechism—
Vatican Council II**

Introduction

As Saint Augustine was walking on the beach, pondering the mystery of the Trinity, he chanced upon a little child scooping water into a tiny vessel. "What are you doing?" he asked. "I'm putting the sea into this cup," replied the child. "But don't you know that's impossible?" Augustine noted. "Neither can you put the mystery of the Trinity into your head," responded the child. And he vanished.

This story proves an important point about belief and faith. The nature of God is a mystery we humans cannot comprehend. We learn about God only through the ways He reveals Himself: the Scriptures, Jesus' life and mission, the teachings of the Church, and in His personal revelation to us in our experiences.

When you ask a Catholic, "What do you believe?" be ready for a variety of responses. A scholar may quote dogmas and doctrines. Another Catholic may recite the Creed. Still another, like my pious, immigrant grandmother, may smile and reply, "I can't say it in words, but I love my faith." The beliefs of a Catholic cover a broad spectrum and must be considered on different levels.

In this chapter, we explore the phenomenon of belief and how it is applied to Catholic truths. We proceed to an overview of how Catholic doctrine came to be formulated. The final part of the chapter, and the most important aspect, deals with the role of faith in the life of a Catholic.

Nature of Belief

Every religion strives to make meaning out of life. Since the concept of God or the supernatural is overwhelming and abstract, a religion's beliefs need to be put into understandable terms if the religion is to survive. The way the faith is expressed is couched in words, poetry, myths, imagery, or analogy—human means with which one can identify. Human expressions make faith reasonable and are ways in which faith is communicated to others. By using the word *Person* in explaining how God manifests Himself in a threefold manner as Father, Son, and Spirit, we articulate the complex mystery of the **Trinity,** although we do not fully understand it.

Beliefs develop out of the need to express religious concepts and the experience of God. They are intellectual expressions of the faith one possesses within one's heart. Because beliefs are human efforts to articulate a spiritual reality, they fall short of the reality itself and, therefore, are limited and open to a variety of interpretations. This tenuous trait of beliefs makes it necessary for authoritative sources to interpret and guide in expressing a religion.

Religious Beliefs and the Catholic Church

The Catholic faith has been passed on from generation to generation in a variety of ways. Some aspects have changed, others are unchangeable, and new interpretations emerge.

Trinity   *The belief in three Persons in one God: Father, Son, and Holy Spirit*

The teaching authority of the Church, called the magisterium, has been the unifying vehicle through which the Catholic faith has been transmitted through the ages. The faith has been set forth in creeds, formulas of faith, dogmas, ecumenical councils, and other doctrinal statements. The magisterium guides and directs.

However, not everything a Catholic believes has been put into written doctrine, nor is every iota of faith included directly in the Scriptures. The whole body of beliefs passed on in the faith life of believers is called **Tradition.** Since the Church is rooted in the teachings of Christ, it has attempted to transmit truths in a way that is faithful to the spirit of the gospel. As time goes on, certain elements have changed in order to make the truths relevant and meaningful. A Catholic realizes one must be able to sift the changeable aspects of faith from the unchangeable essentials.

The sum total of beliefs included in Scripture, Tradition, and in the teaching authority of the Church is the **Deposit of Faith.** Certain truths have become the official teaching of the Church, whether by direct declaration or in long-practiced traditions.

When the pope, as official head of the Church, affirms a belief and speaks *ex cathedra* (from the chair) or **infallibly,** the truth he proclaims is infallible and binds Catholics to believe it. The truth becomes a **dogma.** Dogmas do not drop full-blown from the sky, nor is a dogma the result of a papal inspiration. It has been present as an accepted belief in the Church, but for one reason or another, the Church at some later point declares it formally as an unchangeable, definite truth. Infallibility has only rarely been invoked.

Deposit of Faith   *The sum total of beliefs in Scripture, Tradition, and the teaching authority of the Church*

Dogma   *A truth of the Church revealed by Scripture or contained in Tradition*

Ex Cathedra   *"From the chair"; the expression used to denote an official teaching of the pope which is infallible*

Infallibility   *The ability of the pope or the bishops in union with the pope to speak officially without error in specific circumstances*

Tradition   *The body of revealed truth handed down from the apostles; often refers to truths not spelled out in Scripture*

Other truths which are subject to various interpretations or change, and which explain and aid Catholics in belief are called **doctrines.** These are beliefs that are inherent within the Catholic faith life, but have not been as definitively and authoritatively defined as have dogmas.

Explanations which are the result of theological inquiry or research are theological explanations and are not part of official Church teachings. These aid toward explaining the faith and over the years have proved valuable in clarifying and making faith more meaningful. Catholics must be aware that materials written in the secular press concerning religious issues often are theological opinions and not the official position of the Church.

There is a hierarchy of beliefs in the Catholic faith. Not every truth is of equal importance. For example, the belief that Jesus is the Son of God and saved us is more important than believing that Saint Pachomius is a powerful intercessor in heaven.

Mystery lies at the heart of one's faith. A believing Catholic must rest content that not all of one's religion can be completely understood, for to understand all of God would make us gods.

The truths contained in the **Nicene Creed** form the belief framework built around the deeper reality of what God means for us in our faith. It would be a beneficial exercise to pray the Nicene Creed prayerfully and reflectively. The discovery of insights, that up to now we have taken for granted, may be a new revelation to us.

Evolution of Catholic Beliefs

In order to understand the changeable and unchangeable aspects of faith, it is an interesting study to trace the formation of doctrine through the ages. Dogmas and doctrines developed in certain historical circumstances. We can distinguish six specific phases:

1. *Early Christian Era* (A.D. 100–300)
Faith was simple for the early Christians. "Reform and be baptized, each one of you, in the name of Jesus Christ." (Acts 2:38)

Doctrine   *A general term referring to the teachings of the Church over and above dogmas*

Nicene Creed   *The formula of chief doctrines of the Catholic Church formulated by a council of the Church*

These basic requirements were marked with a commitment for which many of them gave their lives.

As the faith spread, new converts were instructed through the **kerygma,** the proclamation of who Christ really was, as found in Acts 10:34–43. Later, a simple formula, developed from early apostolic teaching, served as a catechetical tool. It was the basis for the **Apostles' Creed.**

2. *Age of Doctrinal Formulations and Heresies* (A.D. 300–500)

The fervor of the early Christians gave way to an attempt to explain who Jesus was. The human terms used to define the mission of Jesus and his relation to the Father were open to various interpretations.

Conflicting explanations gave rise to heresies. In order to preserve the faith and to clarify beliefs, the ecumenical councils held at Ephesus, Constantinople, and Nicaea defined the basic Christian truths about God, the Trinity, the mission and identity of Jesus, the Church, and Mary as Mother of God. The Nicene Creed capsulizes these fundamental beliefs in the profession of faith recited and accepted by all Christians. Dogmatic formulations were standardized, and Saint Augustine compiled a compendium of truths which gave further theological explanations. For example, he coined the term *original sin* as a way to explain humanity's innate tendency to evil.

3. *Middle Ages* (A.D. 1200–1500)

After the East split from the West to form the Orthodox branch of Christianity, basic theological differences in interpreting beliefs lessened. The West now concentrated on presenting the faith in an organized manner.

The Fourth Lateran Council enacted rituals and regulations concerning the sacraments. Other Church disciplines were explained in the light of the Roman legal system, resulting in Canon Law.

Interpretations of the faith, according to the terms of Greek philosophy, fell to the realm of great scholars. **Saint Thomas Aquinas** brilliantly explained the truths of faith in the light of Aristotelian thought in the *Summa Theologica.*

Apostles' Creed　*A profession of faith which is a summary of the truths taught by the apostles*

Kerygma　*The proclamation of the message of salvation*

Saint Thomas Aquinas　*A Dominican saint (d. 1274) who explained the truths of faith in the light of Aristotelian thought in the* Summa Theologica

150

4. *The Reformation* (A.D. 1500–1600)

The split of Western Christianity into many divergent branches is called the "Reformation." Many historical, political, religious, social, and intellectual circumstances brought about this complex historical event. Among the causes which led to the Reformation were: abuses and corruption within the Church, the separation of authentic piety from theology, the rise of nationalism, and the ideologies of individuals, such as Luther, Zwingli, Calvin, and Henry VIII.

5. *The Catholic Church Counter-Reformation* (A.D. 1545–1563)

The Council of Trent as the Catholic Counter-Reformation defended Catholic truths which already had been defined. It also reiterated doctrines, categorized beliefs, and set up specific guidelines to insure the purity of the faith. Those not abiding were pronounced **anathema,** which means "excluded from the kingdom."

The truths of faith were preserved for the faithful and conveyed in definite form. **Catechisms** were developed that explained the faith in compact question-and-answer format. There was an advantage to this style of teaching for that time because it was definite and Catholics knew exactly what the authentic Catholic teaching required of them. Catholics who received their religious formation prior to Vatican II recall learning many of the truths of faith from the *Baltimore Catechism,* the once official catechism for the United States formulated at the **Fourth Plenary Council** in Baltimore in 1884. This rote method, if relied on solely however, left no room for growth and development of one's personal spirituality. Religious truths were frozen into abstract staid formulas and the Catholic faith was equated with intellectual assent and rote memorization.

6. *Vatican Council II* (A.D. 1962–1965)

Catholic beliefs need to be meaningful for modern people. This was the prime aim of ecumenical renewal. Structures and traditions, while useful, gave way to pastoral concerns.

Anathema *A term meaning "excluded from the kingdom"*

Catechism *An explanation of the faith, often in a question-answer format*

Fourth Plenary Council *National gathering of bishops in Baltimore, Maryland, in 1884*

Vatican Council II *1962–1965, an ecumenical council whose aim was to renew the Church*

Vatican II placed its priorities on the Catholic faith as a dynamic, living reality in the world. It revitalized the Church toward a meaningfulness and spontaneity of spirit and away from a sterile intellectualism.

In order to understand the thrust of Vatican II more definitely, it is fitting to present, in essence, an outline of the sixteen documents of Vatican II. They serve as doctrinal guidelines for the Church today, but are flexible in their implementation. (See pages 152–153.)

Role of Faith in the Life of a Catholic

Faith is one of the three theological virtues, bestowed on us by God at baptism. Ultimately, faith is a gift of God who takes the initiative in our lives. God enables us to believe and give ourselves freely to the truths of religion. Sometimes a person will say, "I want to believe, but I can't." They have not received the gift of faith.

Neither can we give faith to another. Parents who have the child baptized and nurture the child's faith provide the basis, and their faith is handed on as a heritage. However, if the faith is not nurtured by the child, if the child does not respond and chooses not to practice religion, the parents cannot fret. They have done their part, if they have provided an atmosphere of faith. But, to grow, faith needs to be developed, and the person needs to freely respond. Faith is like a seed. It requires sustenance, or else it will die.

It is possible for one to go through the motions of religion and still not have faith. Faith goes beyond external observance. It even supercedes intellectual assent. A simple peasant with no formal theology may have greater faith than a cardinal of the Curia. Faith relies on attitudes and values, not on rituals. It colors life and gives spiritual meaning to daily living.

Faith is living what one believes in. It is no facade and is not frozen in lifeless formulas. It is a divine vision. It is there as we clasp the hand of a dying loved one. Faith is in the "I do" of a young couple who pledge their lives to each other. Faith speaks loudly as survivors scrape up their belongings after a devastating tornado. It awaits the verdict of a doctor. Faith is in the child who prays at his or her bedside; it is in the anxiety when one wonders if the paycheck will last the month. Faith is strong in the weak limbs of a stroke patient trying to walk. All of life is flavored and made meaningful in faith. The faith of a believer tries to see God in all that happens. It is one's religion and beliefs in work clothes. Faith does not hesitate to ask questions, nor does it fear doubt, which leads to deeper understanding.

Documents of Vatican II

4 Constitutions—Most solemn—Dogmatic issues
9 Decrees—Practical guidelines—Disciplinary
3 Declarations—Position of Church on an issue

Dogmatic Constitution on the Church	**Nature of the Church as "People of God"—Redefining of mission—Restores Permanent Diaconate**
Dogmatic Constitution on Divine Revelation	**Scripture and Tradition as main sources of revelation—Importance of Word of God**
Constitution on the Sacred Liturgy	**Liturgy as focus of community piety and worship—Liturgical renewal, participation**
Pastoral Constitution on the Church in the Modern World	**Church and World as mutually related—Dignity of all people—Marriage and family, culture, socio-economic, political concerns, peace**
Decree on the Instruments of Social Communication	**Responsibility and challenge of all media—Use of media to promote faith and values**
Decree on Ecumenism	**Encourages Christian unity and respect for other beliefs—Sets forth guidelines for interfaith endeavors**
Decree on Eastern Catholic Churches	**Addressed to Eastern Churches united with Rome—Recognizes diversity of Rites—Need to retain traditions**

Decree on the Bishops' Pastoral Office in the Church	Collegiality of bishops in sharing authority with pope—Calls for synods of bishops
Decree on Priestly Formation	Priestly training responsibility of National Bishops' Conferences—Call for evaluation of seminary curricula
Decree on the Appropriate Renewal of the Religious Life	Religious called to renew and examine relevance in the world and spirit in conformity to gospel values
Decree on the Apostolate of the Laity	Call of laity to holiness—Involvement in Church—Bring gospel to the world
Decree on the Ministry and Life of Priests	Priests called to integrate life with work and spirituality—Pastoral dimension emphasized
Decree on the Church's Missionary Activity	All share in mission work—Evangelization by example more effective than direct tactics
Declaration on Christian Education	Upholds value of education and efforts to develop the mind—Parents have prime responsibility for moral training of their children
Declaration on the Relationship of the Church to Non-Christian Religions	Sacred values of non-Christian religions—Judaism as root of Christianity—Anti-Semitism condemned
Declaration on Religious Freedom	Conscience is norm of morality—Dignity and rights of human person—Discrimination in all forms condemned

Faith, for Catholics living through Vatican II, has not been easy. Changes came fast and if they were not adequately explained, they may have left Catholics confused. But the new emphases and analogies were meant to make faith more real and alive.

The "Pastoral Constitution on the Church in the Modern World" proclaims that the Spirit is working in the world and that people need to respond in faith: "The People of God believes that it is led by the Spirit of the Lord, who fills the earth. Motivated by this faith, it labors to decipher authentic signs of God's presence and purpose. . . . Faith throws a new light on everything, manifests God's design for man's total vocation, and thus directs the mind to solutions which are fully human."[1]

Catholics, in the spirit of Vatican II, need to pray for the Spirit. The **Prayer of Serenity** is suited for Catholics who strive to live the life of faith that Vatican II presents:

"God grant me the serenity to accept the things I cannot change, the courage to change the things I can, and the wisdom to know the difference."

---

1. Walter M. Abbott, S.J., ed. "Pastoral Constitution on the Church in the Modern World," *The Documents of Vatican II* (New York: America Press, 1966), p. 209, article 11.

Prayer of Serenity   *"God grant me the serenity to accept the things I cannot change, the courage to change the things I can, and the wisdom to know the difference."*

XII

What Is the Catholic Attitude toward Other Religions?

**Crusades—Islam—Vatican II
Documents—Judaism—Ecumenism—
Evangelization**

Introduction

As Saint Peter was taking tourists through heaven, there
was much feasting in each of the large rooms which lined
the gilded corridors. As they came to a room which had its
doors closed, Peter advised, "Tiptoe by this one. These are
the Catholics. They think they're the only ones up here."

Not too long ago this anecdote was a fact. Catholics
born into a Catholic household, usually went to a Catholic
school, lived in a Catholic neighborhood, worked and
socialized with Catholics. One was expected to marry a
Catholic so that the tradition would be carried on.

Today, pluralism is an accepted fact. Nationalities and
faiths exist side by side; cultures freely mingle with each

other. To know and understand others' values and beliefs is no intellectual luxury, but a necessity if people are to live in peace and harmony. One of the more revolutionary moves of Vatican II was the evaluation of Catholic attitudes toward other religions.

In this chapter, we capsulize the ecumenical thinking of Vatican II. We examine the Church's stance in history by highlighting significant encounters. We proceed to the Vatican II breakthroughs in ecumenical understanding and what this implies for the ordinary Catholic in dealings with other faiths. The chapter ends with a consideration of the Church and evangelization.

Historical Highlights of Catholicism and Other Religions

From the early days of Christianity, differences of outlook existed within the believing community. Peter believed it was improper for a Jew to associate with a Gentile or to eat forbidden foods. A vision from God convinced Peter that he "should not call any person profane or unclean." (Acts 10:28) An uncircumcised Gentile was brought into the assembly of Christ's first followers, who were Jews. Whether he needed to become a Jew first before being admitted into the community of believers caused great discussion. (See Acts 15.)

The Church has consistently met with opposition from within and without. The Church spread along culturally-diverse lines as evidenced in the formation of Rites and the fourfold Gospel. Variations and disagreements in explaining beliefs and truths led to heresies and schisms—for instance, the Nestorians, Monophysites, and Docetists.

The next great outside rival to Christianity was **Islam.** Founded by **Muhammed** in A.D. 622, it spread rapidly through the Empire. If Charles Martel had not squelched the Moslem raid at Tours in 732, Europe would have succumbed to Islam, and possibly the whole course of Western history would have changed. Our European ancestors probably would have been Moslems.

Islam   *The Moslem religion*

Muhammed   *The founder of the religion of Islam in 622*

Within the Church, ideological differences intensified and, in 1054, the Eastern Church, now known as the Orthodox Church, separated from Rome. Not much later, the **Crusades** (1095–1270) attempted to regain the Holy Land from the Moslem invaders and, in the end, failed in the attempt.

Although the Fourth Lateran Council attempted to unify the Church by codifying its laws, it did not prove tolerant of other religions. The Jews, who for centuries had been forced to live their tradition in ghettos separate from others, were forced to be even more isolated. The Council decreed that Jews be ostracized, and Christians were prohibited by Church law to associate with them. This is an embarrassing part of Church history and one which demands that Christians today offer recompense by love and tolerance.

Many who attempted reform in the Middle Ages were not tolerated. John Hus was burned at the stake for trying to translate the Bible into the language of the people.

By the time of the Reformation, the Catholic Church turned in on itself in rigid intolerance. All other religions were considered false, and to associate with outsiders was tantamount to heresy. Recall the Church's attitude toward mixed marriages.

The closed attitude toward other religions prevailed until Vatican II. Since intolerance was so ingrained after hundreds of years, it was not easy to adopt new ways of thinking. Is it any wonder that Catholics did not slip into the ecumenical movement as easily as donning a new coat? Rather, it was like forcing oneself into new shoes. There would be much pinching and many blisters before one felt comfortable.

Breakthroughs in ecumenical understanding of Vatican II led to greater tolerance and openness among religions. While pluralism is still not universally and equally accepted by Catholics, many people breathe the air of ecumenism more freely and are comfortable in interfaith endeavors. But there does exist some confusion as to what the thinking of the Church really is regarding ecumenical tolerance.

Several documents of Vatican II deal specifically with ecumenical interests. The "Declaration on Religious Freedom" upholds the dignity of the human person and respects the choices one makes regarding religion as he or she practices it. "[Religious] freedom means that all

Crusades *Military attempts to regain the Holy Land and stop the spread of Islam (1095–1270)*

158

men are to be immune from coercion . . . [and] that in matters religious no one is forced to act in a manner contrary to his own beliefs."[1]

The "Dogmatic Constitution on the Church" defines and makes a distinction which is crucial to Catholic identity and the Church's self-understanding. The document distinguishes between the "Church of Christ" which encompasses all the ecclesial communities following Christ, and the "Catholic Church," which possesses institutional fullness through the pope and bishops. The Church of Christ, "constituted and organized in the world as a society, subsists in the Catholic Church, which is governed by the successor of Peter . . . ."[2] It asserts that the Church of Christ is a larger reality than the visible Catholic Church. This revolutionary attitude acknowledges that "elements of sanctification and of truth can be found outside of her visible structure . . . [and these] possess an inner dynamism toward Catholic unity."[3]

Although the fullness of Christ's revelation is found within the Catholic Church because of its unbroken continuity with Christian origins, the Council recognizes the existence of the message of Christ alive in other ecclesial communities. This shift in understanding requires Catholics to recognize the value in other religions and not to consider them heretical and false.

The Council extends its ecumenical stance by encouraging open dialogue between Christians through interfaith prayer and sharing of faith experiences. The "Decree on Ecumenism" offers practical guidelines and principles, cautioning that the work of the Spirit not be hindered.

The Church is not only concerned about restoring unity among Christians, but in the "Declaration on the Relationship of the Church to Non-Christian Religions," it recognizes that "other religions . . . strive variously to answer the restless searchings of the human heart"[4]

1. Walter M. Abbott, S.J., ed. "Declaration on Religious Freedom," *The Documents of Vatican II* (New York: America Press, 1966), pp. 678–679, article 2.

2. Walter M. Abbott, S.J., ed. "Dogmatic Constitution on the Church," *The Documents of Vatican II* (New York: America Press, 1966), p. 23, article 8.

3. Ibid.

4. Walter M. Abbott, S.J., ed. "Declaration on the Relationship of the Church to Non-Christian Religions," *The Documents of Vatican II* (New York: America Press, 1966), p. 662, article 2.

and point to divinity and grace. It cites spiritual values found in Hinduism, Buddhism, and Islam. "The Catholic Church rejects nothing which is true and holy in these religions."[5] Judaism as the basis and root of Christianity is extolled, and the common heritage shared with Christians is recognized. The Council deplores all forms of anti-Semitism of the past and deeply regrets discrimination, which is opposed to the mind of Christ and the Church.

Fruits of Ecumenical Openness and Dialogue

Formal theological dialogues have become more prevalent with the growth of ecumenical understanding. Interfaith dialogues among Catholics, Lutherans, and Anglicans concerning sacramental theology have flourished as have Christian-Jewish relations. Commissions and offices for unity and interfaith relations have been set up on the Vatican, national, and diocesan levels. A common Bible, in which scholars from various religious persuasions have lent their expertise, has been published. Pope John Paul II continues his example of active ecumenical witness in every country he visits, by meeting with leaders of all religions. He also encourages active dialogue.

While ecumenical endeavors at the highest level are dramatic and impressive, the same spirit must filter into the grass roots. On the local level, parishes have cooperated with other Churches in prayer services, facility sharing, and covenant relationships drawn up to foster a spirit of unity. Catholics are free to join with friends at funerals, weddings, Church services, and other joint endeavors. The Catholic Church's attitude toward mixed marriages has dramatically improved. The Catholic charismatic movement, which thrives as a catalyst for personal, spiritual witness, has received positive impetus from Protestant Pentecostals and their understanding of the life in the Holy Spirit. Catholics, Protestants, and Jews have worked side by side in causes for common concern and joined in prayer together for justice and peace among all peoples.

Ecumenical thinking proves that Catholics can live their faith and tradition loyally while being open and receptive to others' beliefs and values. This attitude does not call for a mere passive acceptance but demands that Catholics reach out in active dialogue and enrich their faith through a broadening of religious perspectives.

---

5. Ibid.

A spirit of tolerance must penetrate into the minds and hearts of every Catholic. How one can adapt his or her thinking according to the spirit of Vatican II in this regard may demand a shift in attitude. The following reflection offers guidelines toward an authentic ecumenical openness.

How to Foster an Ecumenical Spirit in One's Faith Life

A Protestant minister, Catholic priest, and Jewish Rabbi served as chaplains in the same unit in World War II. They pledged if any of them died in battle, the other two would preside at the burial. The rabbi was killed during the invasion of Normandy. True to their word, the two chaplains sought to find a proper burial site. Since there was no Jewish cemetery, they approached the local pastor and asked if they could bury their dead comrade in the parish cemetery. "Let me first check the books," he replied. After consulting the rules, the pastor noted, "He can't be buried within the cemetery, but he can be laid outside the gate." There was no choice, and the rabbi was buried there. Years later, the two chaplains decided to visit the grave. But they could not find it. They asked the aging pastor and he answered, "I used to look at that grave—so alone and cold. I went to the books. In no place did it state that I couldn't move the fence. And that's what I did."

Fences

Before one fully enters ecumenical dialogue or talks to another about their religion, one may have to move some "fences." There is the fence of exclusiveness. One's own ideas are not always the only ones, nor may they be the best. God shares His gifts as He will. It is surprising to some that spiritual values may be found in other religions besides their own.

The fence of stereotypes interferes in one's objective attitude toward other religions. We cannot generalize about an individual or a group. For instance, not all Jews eat only kosher food, not all Catholics say the rosary, nor do all Hindus bathe in the Ganges.

The most subtle of fences is prejudice. Ideas ingrained deep in one's psyche remain latent until an opportune moment. Prejudice involves a resentment against someone or some idea. Although the feeling seems passive, it flares up and can become outright hatred.

Prejudices are born from ignorance. The more we know about another's way of thinking, the more tolerant and understanding we become. A bumper sticker message says it well, "It's easy to 'down' what you're not 'up' on."

Bridges

The fences need to be replaced with bridges of acceptance, understanding, and tolerance. Tolerance is not passive; it is an active attempt to overcome a closed attitude. We need to see another's beliefs as they do. What another person considers sacred and holy demands respect simply because it is holy. Our watchword in dealing with religious beliefs must be: "The believer is always right," even if the way the person expresses his or her faith seems odd and strange. Nothing can replace a sincere heart that reaches out in faith to the Divine.

If you are attentive to the way others interpret the Spirit working in their lives, you may experience a graced moment, and new dimensions of God in your own life will surface. When you step into another's belief system, not for idle curiosity or intellectual satisfaction, but in openness and interest, you become enriched in your own faith.

Raimundo Panikkar speaks of this "intra-religious dialogue" as "a dynamic of itself which discloses another religious world in our neighbor that we can't ignore or brush aside, but we must take it up and integrate it into our own faith."[6]

I recall participating in a Hindu's morning "puja" worship. As Saroj, dressed in her finest sari, prayed, incensed, and bathed the statuettes, I knelt by in rapt wonder. Although the ritual was strange, and since Saroj recited the prayers in Sanskrit, I felt I was on sacred ground, and God was so near.

Lillian Carter wrote from India while she was a Peace Corps volunteer, "The Hindu prays to his god, and mine answers."

Your faith is enriched when you see God alive in so many ways. But one's faith must be open enough, naked enough, and sincere enough to allow another's belief to enter without a thought of being overtaken. If you have a true ecumenical attitude, you can swim in the faith pool of the other, buoyed up with the life jacket of your own beliefs and values. You go with the tide, floating freely without being submerged, and come out vital and refreshed. Sharing another's faith world can be a powerful boost in one's own faith, because you reflect on your own values.

---

6. Raimundo Panikkar, *The Intra-Religious Dialogue* (New York: Paulist Press, 1978).

We can learn from Mahatma Gandhi: "I open all my doors and windows, and allow all cultures and religions to blow about freely, but I refuse to be swept off my feet by any."

Unplanned and unforeseen occasions provide opportunities at unexpected moments: while riding a bus, in line at the supermarket, or on the street. Casual encounters prove more beneficial than structured agendas. Although an ordinary Catholic may feel incompetent for serious in-depth theological discussions, one ought to be conversant enough to be able to share one's faith convictions.

A true ecumenical spirit is one which understands that religious differences and biases exist and sensitive issues cause friction. Most religious differences are based on interpretations and viewpoint, rather than on animosity. Most religions, too, have more points on which they agree than those on which they disagree.

We need to be open and aware of all the human quests for the spiritual, to discover the many faces of God. To be indifferent to humanity's religious quest is to be silent and deaf to God who speaks loudly of His presence through all religions. Religious differences are not as disastrous as religious indifference. We must see divinity splashed throughout the earth in many human expressions. To be truly and authentically "Catholic" is to be universal in the fullest sense of the term; it is to be open to the truth and goodness of God . . . from wherever it comes.

The Catholic Church as Missionary

The Church has always been and will continue to be a "missionary" Church. It has taken the command of Christ to "make disciples of all the nations" most seriously. (Matthew 28:19) With the Vatican II self-evaluation of the nature of the Church, comes a fresh approach to mission activities and attitudes.

"Converting" today does not necessarily mean bringing whole peoples into the Church, baptizing, and dispensing the sacraments. Conversion ultimately is a call to a change of heart. To convert means to live such an attractive faith life, that others are drawn to and encouraged in their own faith commitment. Others are attracted to faith by example and not by direct tactics. It is more accurate to speak of **evangelization** than outright conversion. Another is drawn toward a deeper spiritual life, rather than being brought into a specific denomination or Church.

To evangelize, one draws others by living the gospel fully. You may be the only Bible someone ever reads. The bishops' pastoral on world mission stresses the importance of witness: "Mission is characterized not by power and the need to dominate, but by a deep concern for the salvation of others and a profound respect for the ways that they have already searched for and experienced God."[7]

The effort of evangelization in the Catholic Church aims first to bring back the many lapsed Catholics, those who were baptized in the Catholic faith, but who are not active in their religion. Evangelization extends invitations and is open to aid those who have no religious commitment.

Evangelization does not uproot one from a sincere religious commitment and transplant one into another religion. Such an evangelization is contrary to the thinking of the Church. Catholics respect what others call holy. True mission work attempts to bring and draw the godliness out of people, rather than pour religion into them.

People need to look at each other with openness and respect, so that the world may be one of peace and love. That is ultimately what Christ meant when he prayed that "all may be one." (John 17:21) This is not necessarily total uniformity, but all joined as one spirit, enriching each other with the diversity of faith. The promise of Christ, "Where two or three are gathered in my name, there am I in their midst," applies to all interfaith encounters. (Matthew 18:20) It is not necessary that we all sing the same song, but the music we make ought to blend into a harmony of peace, understanding, and love.

7. National Conference of Catholic Bishops, *To the Ends of the Earth* (Washington, D.C.: United States Catholic Conference, 1986), p. 11.

Evangelization   *The process of proclaiming and helping to bring about the Kingdom of God*

Addenda

Catholicism—
Historical Highlights

100–500

Formation of New Testament 50–100

Spread of Christianity

Persecutions 64–305

Edict of Milan 313, Constantine

Heresies—Councils

Formulation of Creeds

Catechumenate

Doctrines proclaimed ·

Church organization

East vs. West

Augustine 354–430

Barbarians 375–568

Jerome 420, Latin Vulgate

St. Patrick 461

Fall of Rome 476

500–1000

"DARK AGES"

Gregory the Great 590–604, Liturgical reforms

Faith spread into Europe

Islam founded 622

Battle of Tours, 732, quells Islam

Feudalism—Clergy and Nobles vs. Laity

Charlemagne 800

Morality plays

Feast days

Shrines

Pilgrimages

1000–1500

Orthodox Church 1054

Monastic Reforms, 700 monasteries in Europe

Crusades 1096–1274, Christians and Moslems fight for Holy Land

Francis of Assisi 1210

Fourth Lateran Council 1215

Dominic 1215

Thomas Aquinas 1274

Popes in Avignon 1309–1377

"Western Schism" 1378–1418, Dispute over papacy

Popular Piety, Devotions

Renaissance, art—culture

"Renaissance Popes" 1447–1521

Fall of Byzantium 1453

1500–1800

Spanish Inquisition 1479–1700

Protestant Reformation 1517
Luther—Germany
Calvin—France, Switzerland
Henry VIII—England

Catholic "Counter-Reformation," Council of Trent
1543–1565, Jesuits founded by Ignatius Loyola

Founding of active religious congregations

Reforms of Trent enforced

Seminaries—Charles Borromeo (1538–1584)

French Revolution 1789

1800–1900

"Great Awakening" 1830

Denominations multiply in United States

Dogma of Immaculate Conception 1854

Vatican I 1870, Infallibility proclaimed

Height of immigration to United States, Rise of ethnic
parishes and parochial schools 1880–1920

St. Pius X, Frequent Communion 1910

Lateran Treaty 1929, Vatican—independent nation

Biblical scholarship—Form criticism

Dogma of Assumption 1950

American saints: Mothers F. Cabrini and Elizabeth
Seton and Bishop John Neumann

Vatican II 1962–1965, Open—Flexible—Ecumenical

1967—Diaconate

Pope John Paul II, "Pilgrim Pope"

Code of Canon Law (revised) 1983

Reflection of a Catholic in the Spirit of Vatican II

Lord, I've been baptized and been graced by the gift of the Catholic faith. I've tried to live my life in accordance with what I've been taught. But as I look at our Church, how it grew from a small intimate community of believers into an almost giant monolith, I become frightened. Is it the same faith? Or is it the same Christ in our twentieth century? I believe Christ is here today, answering the needs of all, just as he did so long ago. But sometimes I'm overwhelmed by the human element I see. Help me to remember that the Church is people and, as long as we live, there will be shortcomings; there will be limitations; there will be flaws.

Help me at those moments when I get depressed to make an evermore intense attempt to be a sign to the world. I want to show you, Christ, no longer in your physical form, but present through your Church and your people. I need to be you, to mirror in my life your ways. As I develop my personal relationship with you, through a deep prayer life, aid me to emulate your attitudes. I need to be understanding toward those different from my ways. Tolerance ought to be part of my daily schedule.

Let me give you due worship by my attentive and devout involvement in your perfect gift to the Father, the liturgy. It becomes my gift, too.

Lord, let me live in your Church guided by the Spirit to be a sign today, keeping alive your command: "Make disciples of all."

Glossary

Abraham—*The father of the Jewish people, traditionally understood to be the earliest ancestor, with his wife Sarah, of the Hebrews or Israelites*

Advent—*The liturgical season which begins four Sundays before Christmas*

Alb—*Long, loose white robe with full sleeves worn under the chasuble by the priest and deacon at Mass*

Alexandrian Canon—*The collection of Hebrew Scriptures translated into Greek; Septuagint*

Alexandrian Rite—*Early Eastern Rite based in Alexandria in Egypt*

Altar Servers—*Those who assist the priest at Mass, such as helping to prepare the altar*

Anathema—*A term meaning "excluded from the kingdom"*

Angelico, Fra—*Dominican monk and Italian painter of important religious works (1387–1455)*

Angelus Bell—*The ringing of the Church bell at 6 A.M., noon, and 6 P.M. to call people to a special prayer in honor of Mary*

Annulment—*The declaration that a marriage is null and void because it was never validly entered into, due to an invalidating impediment*

Anointing with Oil—*An external sign used in several sacraments: baptism, confirmation, holy orders, and anointing of the sick*

Antiochian Rite—*Early Eastern Rite based in Antioch in Syria (Asia Minor)*

Apocalypse—*Book of Revelation in the New Testament*

Apocrypha—*Seven books of the Old Testament that were in the Septuagint and are in the Catholic versions of the Bible, but not officially in Protestant versions*

Apostles' Creed—*A profession of faith which is a summary of the truths taught by the apostles*

Apostolic Delegate—*A papal representative with no diplomatic status*

Apostolic Nuncio—*Ambassador from the Vatican assigned to a predominantly Catholic country*

Apostolic Pronuncio—*Ambassador from the Vatican assigned to a country which is not predominantly or officially Catholic*

Apparition—*An appearance by Jesus, Mary, saints, or angels to individuals or groups; the Church thoroughly investigates claimed apparitions and approves a few of them that bear the marks of being authentic*

Archbishop—*Usually the bishop of an archdiocese*

Archdiocese—*Usually a metropolitan see, the principal see in a province of dioceses*

Ascension Day—*Feast recalling Jesus' return to the Father forty days after the resurrection, celebrated forty days after Easter*

Ashes—*A sacramental made from palms of the previous year and used to mark the forehead in the sign of the cross on Ash Wednesday*

Ash Wednesday—*The first day of Lent, a day of fast and abstinence*

Assumption—*The dogma concerning Mary being assumed into heaven after death, body and soul*

Assumption, Feast of the—*August 15; recalls Mary's assumption into heaven*

Auxiliary Bishop—*Assistant bishop in a diocese with no right of succession*

Baptistry—*The place for administering baptisms, often near an entrance to a church or near the sanctuary and altar*

Barnabas—*Missionary companion of St. Paul*

Baruch—*Old Testament book not part of the Protestant versions, one of the Apocrypha*

Beatification—*One of the official steps in the canonization process; the person who is beatified is called "Blessed"*

Beatitudes—*A list of blessings included in the Sermon on the Mount in Matthew's Gospel, with variations in Luke's Gospel*

Benediction—*A Eucharistic devotion which includes the exposition of the Blessed Sacrament in a monstrance*

Bernini, Gian Lorenzo—*Italian sculptor of the baroque style with many religious works (1598–1680)*

Bible—*The Sacred Scriptures, Old and New Testaments; the Word of God*

Blessing—*A prayer, usually by a cleric, to invoke God's favor on persons or things*

Book of Kells—*Illuminated Latin manuscript of the four Gospels and related material, produced between the mid-700s and the early 800s in an Irish monastery*

Book of Revelation—*Apocalypse; highly symbolic and secretive book which closes the New Testament*

Breviary—*The liturgical book containing the Divine Office*

Bull of Canonization—*Official proclamation that a person is a saint*

Byzantine Rite—*Early Eastern Rite based in Byzantium (Constantinople), Greece*

Campus Minister—*A priest, religious, or lay person serving the spiritual needs at a college*

Cana—*The site of Jesus' first miracle when he changed water into wine at a wedding feast*

Candlemas Day—*February 2, the day on which candles are blessed*

Candles, Blessed—*Sacramentals used in the liturgy of the Church*

Canonization—*The official Church process by which a person is declared a saint of the Catholic Church*

Capital Sins—*The seven main sources or roots of sin: pride, covetousness, lust, anger, gluttony, envy, and sloth*

Cardinal—*A bishop of high rank, an elector of the pope (until age eighty), a "Prince of the Church"*

Carmelites—*Contemplative religious communities of men and of women*

Catechism—*An explanation of the faith, often in a question-answer format*

Catechist—*A person who teaches religion in parochial schools, parish religion programs, RCIA, and so forth*

Catechumenate—*Period of preparation for the baptism of adults, sometimes of children*

Cathedral—*Principal church of a diocese, where the bishop has his seat*

Celebrant—*The priest celebrating a Mass*

Celibacy—*The chosen unmarried state of life required of priests in the Roman Catholic Church*

Centering Prayer—*A type of contemplation in which the person directs all of his or her energy inward*

Chalice—*Cup used to hold wine during Mass*

Chancellor—*Notary of a diocese*

Chancery—*The office of administration for a diocese*

Chaplain—*A priest appointed for the pastoral service of an institution, hospital, division of the military, religious community, or various groups of the faithful*

Chasuble—*Flowing outer garment worn by the priest at Mass*

Chi-Rho— ☧ *or* ☧ *; Greek symbol for Christ*

Chrism—*Oil blessed by the bishop and used in the administering of several sacraments*

Chrismation—*Confirmation in the Eastern Rite Churches, received with baptism and first Eucharist*

Christian Scriptures—*The books of the New Testament in the Bible*

Church Calendar/Church Year—*The liturgical cycle of seasons and feasts*

Ciborium—*Cup-like vessel used to hold hosts at Mass*

Coadjutor Bishop—*Assistant bishop in a diocese with the right of succession*

College of Cardinals—*The cardinals of the entire Church; a cardinal is called a "Prince of the Church" and is an elector of the Church unless retired (age eighty)*

Collegiality—*The union of all the world's bishops with the pope; often refers to the decision-making power of this group*

Communion of Saints—*The spiritual union among the saints in heaven, the souls in purgatory, and the faithful on earth*

Communion Rail—*A previously used kneeler between the sanctuary and nave of a church*

Concelebrants—*The priests celebrating a Mass together*

Concelebration—*The simultaneous celebration of Mass by more than one priest, consecrating the same bread and wine*

Confessional—*Darkened alcove in a church for confession with a screen between the priest and penitent*

Constantine—*Roman emperor who gave religious freedom to Christians in* A.D. *313*

Contemplation—*The prayer of quiet, an intimate being-with the Lord*

Contemplative Religious Community—*Religious life lived in secluded monasteries; prayer forms the center of the life and work*

Convent—*Residence for women religious*

Cope—*A cape-type vestment used for some religious ceremonies other than Mass*

Corporal—*Square linen cloth placed on altar under chalice and ciborium at Mass*

Corporal Works of Mercy—*Seven charitable works encouraged by the Church*

Council of Nicaea—*Council held in 787 which rejected iconoclasm and the heresy of adoptionism*

Cremation—*The burning of human remains, once strictly forbidden by the Church when it was seen as a denial of immortality*

Crosier—*Bishop's staff or walking stick, an insignia of the episcopal office*

Cross—*Generally refers to the cross without the image of Jesus*

Crucifix—*The cross with the image of Jesus crucified on it*

Cruets—*Small pitchers to hold wine and water at Mass*

Crusades—*Military attempts to regain the Holy Land and stop the spread of Islam (1095–1270)*

Cursillo—*A religious experience weekend begun in Spain whose goal is to change the world by remaking it according to the mind of Christ*

Da Vinci, Leonardo—*Italian Renaissance painter (1452–1519) with many important religious pieces to his credit*

Deposit of Faith—*The sum total of beliefs in Scripture, Tradition, and the teaching authority of the Church*

Diaconate—*The first of the major orders of holy orders, received prior to ordination to the priesthood (transitional diaconate) or with the intent to remain a deacon (permanent diaconate)*

Diocese—*The territory under the jurisdiction of a bishop*

Director of Religious Education—*(DRE) or Coordinator (CRE); person who directs the religious education programs of a parish*

Divine Liturgy—*The main act of worship in Eastern Rite (Catholic and Orthodox) Churches*

Divine Office—*The public, official, and common prayer of the Church*

Divine Praises—*A litany of praises said after Benediction of the Blessed Sacrament*

Divorce—*The dissolution of a marriage*

Doctrine—*A general term referring to the teachings of the Church over and above dogmas*

Dogma—*A truth of the Church revealed by Scripture or contained in Tradition*

Eastern Orthodox Church—*Church of the East more or less centered in Constantinople, not in union with Rome*

Eastern Rites—*Catholic Churches in union with Rome, but having liturgies and prayers specific to the particular Rite*

Ecclesiasticus—*Old Testament book, also called Sirach*

Ecumenical—*Promoting unity among Christians*

Edict of Milan—*Decree by Emperor Constantine granting religious freedom to Christians*

Eparch—*Bishop of an eparchate*

Eparchate/Eparchy—*Eastern Church diocese*

Epistles—*Early letters of the Christian Church included in the Christian Scriptures*

Eucharist—*1. The liturgy of the Mass; 2. Communion or the Sacrament of (Communion); 3. The consecrated bread and wine; 4. Thanksgiving*

Eucharistic Minister—*A person who distributes Communion at Mass or who takes Communion to the homebound or those in hospitals and nursing homes*

Evangelization—*The process of proclaiming and helping to bring about the Kingdom of God*

Ex Cathedra—*"From the chair"; the expression used to denote an official teaching of the pope which is infallible*

Extreme Unction—*A previously used term for the Sacrament of Anointing of the Sick*

Faculties—*The right a priest has to exercise his priestly office within the diocese*

Fatima—*Shrine in Portugal, a place of miracles dating back to the early part of the twentieth century; related to an apparition of Mary*

Forty Hours' Devotion—*A solemn exposition of the Blessed Sacrament for a period of forty hours*

Fourth Lateran Council—*The "Great Council," gathering of the pope and bishops in Rome in 1215; established Easter Communion practice, initiated a four-year truce for Christian nations, organized the College of Cardinals*

Fourth Plenary Council—*National gathering of bishops in Baltimore, Maryland, in 1884*

Francis of Assisi—*A saint from Italy who lived 1182–1226, founder of the Franciscan mendicant order*

Fruits of the Spirit—*Twelve virtues related to the work of the Holy Spirit in people*

Fundamentalists—*Generally refers to those who adhere to a literal interpretation of the Bible*

Fundamental Option—*The life choice a person makes toward or away from God; this life choice is reinforced by a pattern of behavior*

General Absolution—*The form of sacramental forgiveness of sins given when individual confession by a large number of people is not possible*

Genuflection—*A brief kneeling on the right knee as a sign of respect before the Blessed Sacrament*

Gifts of the Spirit—*Seven virtues related to the work of the Holy Spirit in people*

Gospel of John—*A proclamation of the Good News of Jesus to the people of Ephesus, included in the New Testament*

Gospel of Luke—*A proclamation of the Good News of Jesus to the people of Antioch, included in the New Testament*

Gospel of Mark—*A proclamation of the Good News of Jesus to the people of Rome, included in the New Testament*

Gospel of Matthew—*A proclamation of the Good News of Jesus to the people of Jerusalem, included in the New Testament*

Gospels—*Proclamations of the Good News of Jesus; four are included in the New Testament*

Grace—*God's life in a person; a free gift*

Gregorian Chant—*Church music dating back to the sixth century; one-voice, vocal plainsong—sung without organ*

Habit—*Distinctive clothing of a religious man or woman*

Hail Mary—*A common prayer in praise of Mary asking for her intercession*

Hebrew Scriptures—*The Old Testament of the Bible*

Hell—*The state of eternal rejection of God*

Holy Days of Obligation—*Days on which Catholics are required to participate in the celebration of Mass; in addition to Sundays, there are six in the United States: Christmas, the Solemnity of Mary (January 1), Ascension (forty days after Easter), Assumption of Mary (August 15), All Saints (November 1), and Immaculate Conception (December 8)*

Holy Orders—*The sacrament by which a deacon, priest, or bishop is ordained*

Host—*Bread used at Mass*

Hymnal—*Book of hymns used in church*

Icon—*Two-dimensional religious painting proper to the Eastern Rite Churches*

Iconoclasm—*The heresy which condemned any use of statues or other representations of Christ, Mary, the angels, and saints*

Iconostasis—*Large, wooden screen painted with icons; separates the nave from the sanctuary in many Eastern Rite churches*

Immaculate Conception, Feast of the—*December 8; recalls the belief that Mary was conceived without sin*

Indulgence—*The remission of temporal punishment due for sins*

Infallibility—*The ability of the pope or the bishops in union with the pope to speak officially without error in specific circumstances*

Islam—*The Moslem religion*

Israelites—*The Jewish people; commonly used term in the Old Testament*

Jeremiah—*Old Testament prophet of Judah who preached the love of God; a major prophet*

Jesuits—*Society of Jesus, a religious order of men founded in 1534 by Saint Ignatius of Loyola*

Jesus Prayer—*A common Eastern Rite prayer: Lord, Jesus, be merciful to me, a sinner*

Judith—*Old Testament book not part of the Protestant versions, one of the Apocrypha*

Kerygma—*The proclamation of the message of salvation*

Laicization—*The process by which a priest is returned to the status of a lay person*

Last Rites—*The Sacraments of Reconciliation, Eucharist, and Anointing given to a dying person; the term itself is no longer officially used by the Church*

Latin Rite—*Western or Roman Rite of the Catholic Church; Catholic Churches with the Roman liturgy*

Lectern—*The reading stand used in church*

Lectionary—*The book of Scripture readings used at Mass*

Lector—*The person who proclaims the first two Scripture readings at the Sunday Mass or the first reading at a weekday Mass*

Lent—*The six plus weeks from Ash Wednesday to the celebration of the Lord's Supper on Holy Thursday; a liturgical season of preparation for Easter*

Limbo—*A term used in the Middle Ages and later in an attempt to explain the eternal destiny of unbaptized children who died; a state of natural and eternal happiness*

Lourdes—*Shrine in France, a place of miracles dating back to the latter part of the nineteenth century; related to an apparition of Mary*

Love—*Charity and concern for self, others, and God*

Maccabean Era—*A period of time in the second century B.C.E. when the last Old Testament books were first written*

Maccabees—*Two Old Testament books not part of the Protestant versions, two of the Apocrypha*

Magisterium—*The teaching authority of the Church*

Marian Theology—*Church teachings and traditions regarding Mary, the Mother of God*

Marriage Encounter—*A weekend religious experience for married couples which aims to make good marriages better*

Martin Luther—*(d. 1546) Augustinian monk who was eventually responsible for starting the Protestant Reformation; founder of the Lutheran Church*

Maryknoll—*Catholic Foreign Mission Society of America, a religious order founded in 1911*

Matrimony—*The marriage contract celebrated sacramentally*

Mendicants—*Religious orders without property rights whose members worked or begged for their support*

Michelangelo—*Italian sculptor, painter, and architect (1475–1564), responsible for some of the greatest religious art*

Ministry—*Service in or to the Church*

Miracle Play—*Medieval religious dramas meant as teaching aids; preceded morality plays*

Miter—*A hat with peaks in front and back, worn by a bishop at liturgical services*

Monastery—*The dwelling place for a community of monks or nuns*

Monk—*A religious priest or brother of a monastic order, usually living in a monastery*

Monsignor—*An honorary title given to a priest who distinguishes himself by outstanding service*

Monstrance—*An ornate golden vessel used for the exposition of the Blessed Sacrament*

Muhammed— *The founder of the religion of Islam in 622*

National Shrine of the Immaculate Conception— *Important United States shrine in Washington, D.C.*

Natural Law— *The laws which govern the nature of things; the natural moral law refers to proper human action by people*

Nave— *Main body of a church building*

New Testament— *The Christian Scriptures of the Bible*

Nicene Creed— *The formula of chief doctrines of the Catholic Church formulated by a council of the Church*

Novena— *Devotional prayers repeated for nine days or one day a week for nine weeks*

Novitiate— *A formal period of trial and formation for a man or woman preparing for membership in a religious community*

Nuptial Mass— *The Mass at which a marriage is celebrated*

Old Testament— *The books of Hebrew Scriptures found in the Bible*

Ordinary Time— *Time during the Church year not related to specific feasts: the day after the Sunday after January 6 to the day before Ash Wednesday and the day after Pentecost to the day before Advent*

Ordination— *Those rites in which there is a laying on of hands that invests the man with official priestly authority*

Ordo— *Book of directions for the Mass and Divine Office on a daily basis*

Original Sin— *The result of the sin of our first parents which affects all people in its consequences*

Palm Sunday— *The last Sunday of Lent; recalls Jesus entry into Jerusalem*

Papacy— *The office of the pope*

Papal Mass— *A Eucharistic celebration at which the pope presides*

Papal States— *The temporary land holdings of the papacy prior to 1870; the last of the Papal States was formally signed over to Italy in 1929 with the Lateran Concordat*

Parish— *A community of the faithful, generally territorial and centered in a church building*

Parish Council—*Representatives of the laity in a parish who assist the pastor and staff in the overall running of the parish*

Parochial School—*A Catholic school, parish or diocesan owned and administered, sometimes a private school owned and/or administered by a religious community*

Paschal Mystery—*The passion, death, resurrection, and ascension of Christ*

Passion Play at Oberammergau—*A type of miracle play begun in 1633 and continuing to the present*

Pastor—*An ordained minister charged with responsibility for the people committed to his care, for example, a parish priest or the bishop of a diocese*

Paten—*Flat dish to hold the large host (bread) at Mass*

Paul—*Early convert to Christianity, apostle to the Gentiles*

Pectoral Cross—*Cross on a chain worn by a bishop or an abbot as a sign of office*

Penance—*Acts of reparation*

Permanent Diaconate—*The first of the major orders of holy orders*

Persecutions—*Local or general oppression of early Christians*

Pilgrimage—*A prayerful journey to a place of devotion*

Poor Box—*Collection box at church entrance for alms for the less fortunate*

Pope Damasus—*Pope at the time of the Ecumenical Council Constantinople in 381; a saint*

Prayer of Serenity—*"God grant me the serenity to accept the things I cannot change, the courage to change the things I can, and the wisdom to know the difference."*

Precepts of the Church—*Six Church laws governing Catholics*

Priest—*A man who is ordained; officiates at liturgy, administers the sacraments, and ministers to people's spiritual needs*

Province—*An archdiocese and one or more nearby dioceses*

Psalms—*The book of 150 hymn prayers in the Old Testament*

Purgatory—*Place or condition of temporal suffering and punishment for those who have died in the state of grace, but with some attachment to sin*

Raphael—*Great painter of the Italian Renaissance (1483–1520) with a vast number of religious works to his credit*

Real Presence—*Jesus, true God and true man, really and substantially present, in a mysterious way, under the appearances of bread and wine*

Reconciliation Room—*Small room for the celebration of the Sacrament of Reconciliation, set up for face-to-face confession, though a screen is sometimes available*

Rectory—*Residence for priests*

Relic—*Any part of the bodily remains of a saint; items connected to the saint's life, such as clothing*

Religious—*A man or woman, men or women, who belong to a religious community and make vows*

Rite of Christian Initiation of Adults—*The process (stages and rites) by which unbaptized adults are initiated into the Catholic Church*

Roman Catholic Church—*Church of the West centered in Rome when the Eastern Orthodox Church separated*

Roman Curia—*The body of officially organized agencies assisting the pope in governing and administering the Church*

Rosary—*A devotion in honor of Mary and a string of beads used to count the prayers*

Royal Doors—*Gateway to the sanctuary in an iconostasis (wooden screen) in an Eastern Rite church*

Sacramental—*An object, action, or blessing which is a sacred sign of spiritual favors from God*

Sacramentary—*The book used by the priest which contains the order of Mass*

Sacraments of Initiation—*Baptism, confirmation, and Eucharist; the sacraments by which a person is initiated into the Catholic Church*

Sacrarium—*Special sink for washing the sacred vessels used at Mass*

Sacred Congregation for the Causes of Saints—*The office in the Vatican that investigates the lives of people to be declared saints and regulates the process*

Sacristan—*The person who takes care of the sanctuary, sacred vessels, and altar linens*

Sacristy—*A room for the storage of sacred vessels, vestments, and so forth, in a church; sometimes used for vesting*

Saint Augustine—*Saint from Hippo in North Africa, 354–430; a Doctor of the Church whose many writings have greatly influenced the theology of many Christian Churches*

Saint Blaise—*The saint on whose feast day, February 3, Catholics may participate in the sacramental blessing of throats*

Saint Charles Borromeo—*Sixteenth century cardinal and saint who actively promoted the education of the clergy*

Saint Dominic—*Saint of the thirteenth century, founder of the Dominican mendicant order*

Saint Ignatius of Loyola—*Sixteenth century saint, founder of the Society of Jesus (Jesuits), author of* The Book of Spiritual Exercises

Saint Jerome—*The saint who translated the books of the Bible into Latin in the fourth century; called the Vulgate*

Saint Jude—*An apostle, also known as Thaddeus; regarded as the patron of hopeless causes*

Saint Nicholas—*A bishop of Myra known for his charity, giving rise to the story of Santa Claus*

Saint Patrick—*The saint traditionally considered responsible for the conversion of Ireland; his feast day, March 17, is celebrated by Irish everywhere*

Saint Thomas Aquinas—*A Dominican saint (d. 1274) who explained the truths of faith in the light of Aristotelian thought in the* Summa Theologica

Saint Valentine—*The saint whose feast day has become the secular celebration of Valentine's Day, February 14*

Sanctuary—*The portion of the church building that contains the altar*

Sanctuary Lamp—*A candle or lamp that is kept burning before the Blessed Sacrament*

Scapular—*1. A shoulder-wide, long, outer garment which is part of many religious habits; 2. A sacramental, small imitation of the religious habit worn around the neck, usually by specific groups*

Seder Meal—*Jewish feast celebrated in the home with a meal; commemorates the exodus of the Israelites from Egypt; part of the Passover celebration*

Seminary—*A house of study and formation in preparation for the priesthood*

Septuagint—*The Hebrew Scriptures translated into Greek; also called the Alexandrian Canon*

Sermon on the Mount—*Chapters 5–7 of Matthew's Gospel, which includes many of Jesus' teachings*

Sexton—*Infrequently used term for a church maintenance person*

Shrine—*A sacred place associated with a holy person or a supernatural occurrence*

Sign of Peace—*A greeting to those around one during the Communion Rite of the Mass*

Simony—*Buying and selling spiritual goods*

Sirach—*Ecclesiasticus, Old Testament book not part of the Protestant versions, one of the Apocrypha*

Spiritual Works of Mercy—*Seven spiritual charitable works encouraged by the Church*

Sponsor—*1. A godparent at baptism; 2. A person who accompanies another preparing for the Sacraments of Initiation, or for confirmation or marriage*

Stained-glass Windows—*Colorful windows often found in churches; many tell biblical stories or depict saints, others are symbolic*

Stations of the Cross—*A series of meditations on the sufferings, death, and burial of Christ*

Statues—*Three-dimensional representations of Jesus, Mary, the saints, or angels; often found in churches, but away from the main altar*

Stipend—*Monetary offering made to a priest when requesting that a Mass be said for a particular intention or person*

Stole—*Long, narrow strip of cloth; vestment, worn across the shoulders and down the front, by the priest; across one shoulder and attached at the waist on the other side, by the deacon*

Swiss Guards—*The Vatican security force charged with the personal safety of the pope; members wear uniforms designed by Michelangelo*

Tabernacle—*The structure in which the Blessed Sacrament is reserved, sometimes at a side altar or a separate chapel*

Tobias—*Old Testament book not part of the Protestant versions, one of the Apocrypha*

Tradition—*The body of revealed truth handed down from the apostles; often refers to truths not spelled out in Scripture*

Transitional Diaconate—*The first of the major orders of holy orders, received prior to ordination to the priesthood*

Trappists—*Contemplative religious community of men; Trappistines are the women counterparts*

Tridentine Mass—*The Eucharistic liturgy set up by the Council of Trent in the sixteenth century*

Trinity—*The belief in three Persons in one God: Father, Son, and Holy Spirit*

Uniates—*Eastern Rite Churches in union with Rome*

Ushers—*Ministers of hospitality who usually greet those entering the church, collect the offerings, and direct movement at the time of Communion*

Vatican—*The residence of the pope*

Vatican City—*Part of Rome designated by the Lateran Treaty of 1929 as an independent state, it contains the central administration of the Catholic Church and the residence of the pope*

Vatican Council II—*1962–1965, an ecumenical council whose aim was to renew the Church*

Vatican Museums—*Buildings in Vatican City which contain priceless treasures of art from all ages*

Vernacular—*The ordinary language of the people*

Vestibule—*Foyer and entrance to a church*

Viaticum— *The Sacrament of the Eucharist received by a dying person*

Vicar General— *A priest or bishop appointed by the bishop of a diocese to act as his deputy in the diocesan administration*

Vicar of Christ— *A title for the pope*

Virgin Birth— *The Church dogma or belief that Jesus, the Son of God, was born of only one human parent, Mary, and that she did not lose her virginity*

Vulgate— *The Latin translation of the Bible made by Saint Jerome*

Wisdom— *Old Testament book not part of the Protestant versions, one of the Apocrypha*

Bibliography

Abbott, Walter M., S.J., ed. *The Documents of Vatican II*. New York: America Press, 1966.

Anderson, William. *In His Light*. Dubuque, Iowa: Wm. C. Brown Company Publishers, 1985.

Bausch, William J. *A New Look at the Sacraments*. West Mystic, Connecticut: Twenty-Third Publications, 1977.

Canon Law Society. *The Code of Canon Law*. Grand Rapids, Michigan: William B. Eerdmans Publishing Company, 1983.

Champlin, Joseph M. *The Living Parish: A Believing, Caring, Praying People*. Notre Dame, Indiana: Ave Maria Press, 1976.

Cooke, Bernard. *Ministry to Word and Sacraments*. Philadelphia, Pennsylvania: Fortress Press, 1976.

Cunningham, Lawrence. *The Catholic Faith: An Introduction*. New York: Paulist Press, 1987.

Deedy, John. *The Catholic Fact Book*. Chicago, Illinois: Thomas More Press, 1986.

Dolan, John P. *Catholicism: An Historical Survey*. Woodbury, New York: Barron's Educational Series, 1968.

Foley, Leonard, O.F.M. *Believing in Jesus: A Popular Overview of the Catholic Faith*. Cincinnati, Ohio: St. Anthony Messenger Press, 1985.

Foy, Felician, O.F.M., ed. *Catholic Almanac*. Huntington, Indiana: Our Sunday Visitor, 1987.

Fullam, Raymond, S.J. *Exploring Vatican II*. Staten Island, New York: Alba House, 1969.

Hardon, John, S.J. *Modern Catholic Dictionary*. New York: Doubleday, 1979.

Hassan, Bernard. *An American Catholic Catalog*. New York: Harper and Row Publishers, Inc., 1980.

Hellwig, Monika. *Understanding Catholicism*. New York: Paulist Press, 1984.

Martos, Joseph. *Doors to the Sacred: Historical Introduction to the Sacraments in the Catholic Church*. New York: Doubleday, 1981.

McBrien, Richard. *Catholicism*. San Francisco, California: Winston Press, Harper and Row Publishers, Inc., 1981.

McKenzie, John, S.J. *The Roman Catholic Church*. New York: Holt, Rinehart and Winston, 1969.

The New Catholic Encyclopedia. New York: McGraw-Hill, 1966.

The Official Catholic Directory. New York: P. J. Kenedy and Sons, 1987.

Panikkar, R. *The Intra-Religious Dialogue*. New York: Paulist Press, 1978.

Wilkins, Ronald. *Our Church in History*. Dubuque, Iowa: Wm. C. Brown Company Publishers, 1987.

Index

Media Resources for Christian Initiation from BROWN-ROA

The Last Supper
Jesus met with his twelve disciples in the "upper room" where they shared the meal that history knows as the "Last Supper." This video depicts Passover and the events from Palm Sunday through Holy Thursday.

Barnabas: The RCIA Sponsor
Thirty-minute video program moving through each stage of the RCIA detailing a sponsor's skills, qualities, and roles. Several members of a catechumenate team share their experiences, insights, and personal rewards as sponsors.

RCIA: The Journey through Easter
Thirty-minute video program features catechumens from a variety of backgrounds sharing how they first came to participate in the Rite and the feelings, events, and faith experiences during their journeys. Balanced with Scripture readings from the Easter Vigil and information on each of the four stages.

Sacraments of Initiation: How We Become the Church
A 90 minute video with three segments.
1. Understanding Initiation
2. An Appreciation of Baptism from Scripture
3. Rite of Baptism: Its Importance as a Statement of Faith

For more information, contact:

BROWN-ROA

A Division of Harcourt Brace & Company

P. O. Box 1028, Dubuque, IA 52004-1028
1-800-922-7696

Resources for Christian Initiation
from BROWN-ROA

RCIA: The Process
In clear, simple terms, the themes, roles, content for each period, and short informational passages for the different stages of the RCIA and their corresponding celebrations.

Power in the Rite: Celebrating the RCIA
Ten detailed liturgy outlines with accompanying reflection and commentary for use during the RCIA.

In His Light
An adult catechism explaining the what and why of Catholicism plus current thoughts and trends which show the contemporary Church in action.

Journeying in His Light
An adult formation guide with 35 topics and session outlines.

Adult Education Ministry
How to establish a committee for adult education and a proven process to develop an adult education program.

For more information, contact:

BROWN-ROA
A Division of Harcourt Brace & Company

P. O. Box 1028, Dubuque, IA 52004-1028
1-800-922-7696

Resources for Christian Initiation
from BROWN-ROA

RCIA: Foundations of Christian Initiation

Provides a general introduction to Christian Initiation as well as guidelines and starters for its implementation.

RCIA: A Practical Approach to Christian Initiation

Work sheets, program sessions, outlines for the rites, and guidelines for implementing the RCIA.

RCIA: A Total Parish Process

Outlines ways of teaching, training, experiencing, sharing, motivating, and other suggestions which can be implemented for using the RCIA as a source of renewal for the entire parish family.

Step-by-Step: A Catechetical Handbook for the RCIA

Session outlines and resource articles for each of the four stages for parishes just beginning to integrate the RCIA into the whole complex of parish life.

The Way We Were

The script for *Joppa*, a unique, imaginative vignette where everyone participates in forming a faith community, developing a ministry, and interacting with the inquirers.

For more information, contact:

BROWN-ROA
A Division of Harcourt Brace & Company

P. O. Box 1028, Dubuque, IA 52004-1028
1-800-922-7696

Resources for Christian Initiation
from BROWN-ROA

Let the Children Come to Me

Preparation for Christian Initiation for Children of Catechetical Age
A new program available in three levels: primary, intermediate,
and upper. Five components: program manual, catechist guide,
and student booklets for each level.

The program manual contains all the material necessary to
facilitate and teach the program. It discusses the pastoral team
and gives suggested time lines. Several appendices are included with suggestions for parent/godparent program, rites of
election and catechumenal anointing, skills inventory, and
additional resources. The catechist's guide provides the lesson
plans.

The student booklets contain five units to help the young
catechumenate better understand the significance of belonging
to God's family: praying, forgiving, and sharing as Jesus did;
new life in Jesus; and the Sacrament of Baptism itself. The final
unit concludes by showing the links between Baptism and
Confirmation and Eucharist.

Written by Emily F. Filipi, MRE and Rev. Thomas L. Long.

Children's Sunday Liturgies Made Easy

Twenty-eight liturgies for use with children. Includes reproduc-
ible pantomime outlines, homilies, and take-home handouts.
Also includes background information on forming a children's
liturgy committee, music notes, checklist for liturgy chairperson,
and extensive resources bibliography.

For more information, contact:

BROWN-ROA

A Division of Harcourt Brace & Company

P. O. Box 1028, Dubuque, IA 52004-1028
1-800-922-7696